COLLEGE
COUNSELING
for School Counselors

*Delivering Quality, Personalized College Advice
to Every Student on Your (Sometimes Huge) Caseload*

PATRICK J. O'CONNOR, PhD

DENVER, COLORADO

College Counseling for School Counselors
Delivering Quality, Personalized College Advice to Every Student on Your (Sometimes Huge) Caseload

Outskirts Press, Inc.
http://www.outskirtspress.com

ISBN: 978-1-4327-7808-8

Library of Congress Control Number: 2015912896

Outskirts Press and the "OP" logo are trademarks belonging to Outskirts Press, Inc.

PRINTED IN THE UNITED STATES OF AMERICA

Also by Patrick O'Connor

College is Yours in 600 Words or Less

College is Yours 2.0: Preparing, Applying, and Paying for Colleges Perfect for You

College is Yours 3.0: Getting What You Need to Get into College and Get On with Your Life (coming January 2016)

For Dianne, with my heartfelt thanks and love

TABLE OF CONTENTS

ACKNOWLEDGMENTS

Bob Bardwell of Monson High School first brought the issue of college counseling training to a national level. Through his work as chair of an ad hoc committee of the National Association for College Admission Counseling, I started to see a way to meet a need I'd known about for years, but didn't know how to address. Bob shared his college counseling class syllabus with me, and years later, that modified syllabus is now the framework for much of this book. He continues his national leadership in counselor education, all while serving his students with great focus and care.

After several years of trying (and failing) to help Bob spread the word about the need for better training in college counseling, I thought it might be best to let others take up this important work. The energy and vision of Sarah Summerhill of Michigan State University, however, convinced me I had more to do. Without her commitment and persistence, this book would never have been written.

Other colleagues and friends are the inspiration for this book as well. Lori Johnston of East Grand Rapids High School is the ultimate college counseling minute-person, who drops everything to support the efforts expressed in this book. Mike Kolar of Michigan State gave me new energy and opportunities to focus on this work when it was just an idea, as did Jim Cotter, Michigan

State's director of undergraduate admissions, while John Ambrose of Michigan State opened my eyes to why this work is especially important for students in urban and rural areas.

Brandy Johnson of the Michigan College Access Network took the idea of counselor training to heart, and to a level not seen in any other state. The entire MCAN team sets the example of how we can all improve college access, with Jamie Jacobs leading the counselor education effort.

Joyce Smith, David Hawkins, and Mike Rose at NACAC have also played important roles in shaping this book and the course it's based on. Their view of the college counseling world and the political landscape are most appreciated, as are those of Pat Martin, former vice president at the College Board.

Joe Rosener and Patricia Ryan of Learning Disabilities Association of Iowa (LDA) and Clarisse Bolduc of Oakland Community College launched my initial college counseling classes, while Ken Anselment of Lawrence University, Tim Hayden of Baltimore County Public Schools, Judy Hingle of Fairfax Public Schools (now retired), Lucas Inman of Grandville High School, and Christopher Tremblay of Western Michigan University have helped take training in college counseling to audiences who would have otherwise never received it. Christopher deserves additional thanks for dragging me into serving as coeditor of the *Journal of College Access*, a role I now cherish.

Gene Kalb invited me to write a regular column for *High School Counselor Week* a few years ago, and many of the ideas in this book were first shared there, keeping me sharp for the task of assembling them here.

Jessica Fowle of Kalamazoo College was the first college admissions officer to take the course. In doing so, she opened my perspective to a brand new audience in need of this information, and suggested adding chapter fifty-eight, to make sure new school counselors weren't overwhelmed by the contents of this book. Jess also served as an editor of my drafts, along with Dianne O'Connor and Ila O'Connor. Combined, they saved me from many a grammatical blunder, and were a great help in setting the tone of the book.

Additional thanks go to William Dingledine and the members of the commission of the American Institute of Certified Educational Planners, for their commitment to quality counselor education and credentialing; Jon Gubera and Patricia Renner of the College Board, for their advice on college counseling policy at the state and national level; Headmaster Charles Shaw and my colleagues on the Cranbrook Kingswood Upper School college counseling team—Dean Deren Finks, Associate Deans Sheila Bailey, Bill Hancock (who introduced me to the phrase 'überselective college'),Portia Hedgespeth, and Charlene Rencher, Counselor Amanda Miller, and the dynamic administrative staff of Vicki Skok and Maggie Higgins; Randall Dunn, head of Latin School of Chicago; Patricia Bostwick, Bridghette Parker, and Bonnie Schemm of The Roeper School; and the very brave members of the executive board of the Michigan Association for College Admission Counseling.

The ideas expressed in this book are an accumulation of years of insights, interactions, and inspirations from the finest colleagues and friends one could hope for. All they have done for me and for my students goes beyond the bounds of description—my heartfelt thanks for your words and support.

INTRODUCTION

Students and parents need more help investigating colleges than ever before. Students have more college options than their parents did, so they both need help surveying this larger landscape. The days are gone when students working a good summer job could pay for most of their college tuition, so help with college financing is also in order. If you add in the economic impact the right college decision could have on a student's future earnings, the need to make a good, personalized college choice—which could also be a decision not to attend college—is clear for each student, and for our country.

While college options and college costs may have soared, school counselors report they've had trouble meeting the demand for more college counseling. Most counselor caseloads are the highest they've ever been, and tight school budgets are requiring many counselors to devote more of their time to tasks that have little to do with counseling.

These demands put a counselor's college counseling skills to the test, and many counselors report a lack of preparation in college counseling during their graduate school training. Combined, these factors mean counselors are largely left to design, implement, and evaluate this critical service on their own.

This book is designed to help counselors meet this essential need. The first few chapters provide a framework for a comprehensive curriculum in college counseling—one that starts well before high school, and requires the active participation of more than just the college counselor.

The remaining chapters fill out the curricular framework with details on the programs and information that families need to make strong college plans based on the student's interests, talents, and needs. Strategies for bringing the college counseling curriculum to life are designed for counselors with even large caseloads who have limited time for individual student appointments. Emphasis is placed on the knowledge, leadership, coordination, and communication skills the counselor will need to serve as the building leader in college curriculum, without requiring the counselor to be the sole implementer of the curriculum.

Realizing school counselors are busy people, each chapter offers focused information that can be read and reviewed in just a few minutes. Each chapter ends with a Notes and Follow-Up section that includes about thirty minutes of questions, activities, and research counselors can complete to bring the ideas of the chapter to life.

The quick pace makes the book a valuable resource to keep at hand when talking with students, while the Notes and Follow-Up section helps counselors develop the habit of devoting thirty minutes of their professional day to the college counseling curriculum. This time may be hard to find at first, but most counselors realize the value of this habit within a week or two, and look for more ways to keep this half-hour as part of their daily schedule.

There is no better match in school counseling than students who are eager to learn more about themselves and the world around them, and a caring counselor with the skills, strategies, and knowledge to support that goal. *College Counseling for School*

Counselors is the roadmap counselors can use to make the most of that match, creating powerful college exploration opportunities for every student, regardless of counselor caseload.

A Word about Initiating Change

Most counselors pick up books about counseling curriculum and hope to get one or two ideas they can add to their programs right away. Readers of the early drafts of this book report they certainly found those one or two ideas, and then some—so much so that they weren't sure what to do first, once they got to the end of the book.

The best way to maintain focus on the goals for your program is to write them down now, before you start reading. What would be the five areas of college counseling you would want to improve this year, if you had thirty minutes a day to work on curriculum development? With those as your guide, use the ideas in this book to help you affirm, adjust, or abandon those goals, as long as you end up at the end of your reading with a reasonable list of ideas you can bring to life by the end of the school year.

If you're starting a college counseling curriculum from scratch, or looking for some help prioritizing your goals, chapter 58 offers a three-year plan to get most of the ideas in this book off the ground. Start there, and read the relevant chapters in the recommended order if you'd like—but it's really best to set your goals, adjust them as you read the entire book, and then compare your list with chapter 58.

Successful change is sane and manageable, and most counselors feel they're already living at school as it is. Think about your five top goals and go from there.

A Word about Website References

Counselors love websites, and rightfully so. With college trends and admission requirements changing so quickly, access to the latest information is a must—and so is understanding the value of each website in its right context.

Footnotes and end notes don't always make for smooth reading, and putting a full-blown web address in the middle of a paragraph isn't much better. That's why any web reference in this book is in italics; if you type the italicized phrase in a web search, the link to the site will almost undoubtedly be the first result of the search.

Since school counselors are on tight budgets, the products and information on most every website referenced in the book can be accessed for free. The handful of fee-based resources will have an asterisk (*) at the end of the reference. Leave out the * when you're completing the search, and you should find it with ease.

Chapter 1
DATA, AND HOW IT HELPS COUNSELORS HELP STUDENTS

School counselors love to see students, and data plays a big role in making the most of the time counselors have with students in college counseling. If we build a solid framework for the collection, analysis, and use of data, we'll help students make better decisions about college, and help others understand the value of our work. This framework is based on four key questions.

What data do we need to support students in the college selection process?

It's important to remember that no two colleges are alike, and no two students are alike. Part of the joy of our work is matching a student's interests and needs with the programs, services, and environment of the colleges that will best support those interests and needs (and note I said "colleges", not "college.")

Two kinds of data help us find this right "fit" between student and colleges. The first set of data focuses on the student. Grades and test scores are a good start, and easy enough to find in the school databank; so is the student's schedule, which shows the degree of rigor, or how demanding the classes were. It's also helpful to know the student's interests, achievements, life outside of school, the way they simply look at the world, and what they want out of the college experience. This information is best secured through questionnaires or meetings with the student, a process that can be more time consuming, but also more personal.

The second kind of data centers on the colleges. It's easy to learn the average grades and test scores of admitted students, as well as information on the majors, classes, diversity, and student services of a college. Most of this information is available on the college's website, or an online college search tool like *Big Future*. *College Navigator* provides other key data, including the number of students who attend and complete their studies at a college, and how many leave.

This college information is a good start, but it's also good to know how many students from your high school have been admitted to this college, how many attend, and how well they're doing. Every student is different, but if large numbers of your students are doing well at a particular college, that suggests a good fit between the environments of your school and the college for many of your students. On the other hand, if students from your high school aren't performing well, or transfer from a college after a year or two, that may suggest there's something beyond the numbers you need to know in order to advise students accordingly.

Colleges generally have this information, and many are willing to share it with you, if you ask. It's better, and easier, to develop your own set of data on applications and admissions. Many application tracker programs are available, such as *Naviance** or *Guided Path**, and since most include resume builders and interest inventories, they benefit your career counseling efforts as well.

Since FAFSA (Free Application for Federal Student Aid) completion is also a significant indicator of likely college attendance (especially by low-income students), *FAFSA Completion by High School* can show you the percentage of seniors in your high school who have filed a FAFSA, while the *National Student Clearinghouse (NSC)** can help you track your students once they leave high school. This allows you to find out if they went to college, and if so, where they went, and if they finished. Some states can help you track the FAFSA progress of individual students, and some may give you NSC data for free. Be sure to ask.

Notes and Follow-Up

- It's time to get acquainted with your student data sources. Consider where you can find the following data, how easily you can access it, and what role it could play in helping students make college decisions:
  - Grades
  - Absences
  - Discipline
  - Special learning accommodations
  - Free/reduced lunch
  - Feeder schools
  - Colleges where students apply
  - Colleges where students are admitted
  - How students perform in college
  - Scholarships they earn
  - Test scores

Chapter 2
THE DATA OTHERS NEED

The data in chapter 1 helps us do our work, but different data will help others understand our work—and that helps us, too. That's why the second question of our framework is this:

What data do we need to satisfy external audiences?

Counselors aren't the only ones who know the value of data in determining if a high school is successful in helping students make a smooth transition to college. Administrators, state agencies, and local media are eager to receive some of this information and share it with others—and so are parents, including parents of very young students who are looking at a number of different schools or school districts to decide which one will best meet their child's needs.

When preparing and sharing college-related data with others, it's important to keep these key ideas in mind:

Maintain confidentiality. Any data you share with others has to protect the privacy of your students, and that isn't always easy to do. If you keep track of the application success of students by college, it won't be too hard for some members of the public to attach names to the data points of a college admissions scattergram—especially if only a handful of students applied to a particular college. Even when sharing good news—like an individual student who scored well on the ACT or SAT—you need the permission of the student or family before making this public.

Your first duty is always to the student. Keep that in mind as you consider releasing college data. This is especially true when releasing what most people think of as "scholarship" information. If the student says it's OK, it's more than fine to release information about individual awards of merit-based money for college, but it's almost never a good idea to release information about individual need-based awards, since that borders on releasing financial information about parents and students. Announcing need-based aid in the aggregate can help other families realize that financial help for college is available for "families like them," but identifying individual families in need rarely achieves the same goal. Proceed with caution.

Others use data differently. Many people use college-related data to indicate the quality of a counseling department, high school or school district, but there's much more to a successful high school than college readiness—or the number of scholarship dollars the students receive. If you're going to release college data, it's wise to release it in conjunction with other data or descriptors that give a full picture of the department or school's environment (student satisfaction surveys, results of school climate polls, etc.). If you only hand out college data, you'll only be judged by that data. Make the most of the opportunity, and give a full picture of the services of your counseling department, and your school.

Others may want data that is of no real value to you. Since efforts to capture data on college admissions are relatively new, local or state requirements may make you keep track of data that doesn't really help you work with students. In the interest of maintaining good relationships with your administrators (and that's important), you'll want to find a way to track this required information, but share it only with those who require it. If it becomes part of a general report, the public may decide a statistic has meaning when it really doesn't, and that can only weaken your college counseling program.

Notes and Follow-Up

- Take a look at the end-of-the-year report you submit to your principal on your college counseling curriculum (this may double as the school profile you give colleges that summarizes your high school).
  - Does it address anything other than where students are going to college, or how much scholarship money students received?
  - Does it maintain the confidentiality of every student, or is it easy to determine a student's identity from one or more data points?
  - Does it address student or parent satisfaction of the help they received in the college selection process?
- Meet with your principal, and mention you're reviewing the end-of-the-year report. Is there any other information your principal or the school board would like to have about the college counseling curriculum?

- Take a quick online tour of the archives of the local newspaper. What parts of the college counseling curriculum do they cover? Which parts would you like them to cover?

- How well do you know the reporter who covers education in your local paper?

Chapter 3
DATA TRACKING, AND DISAGGREGATION

Now that we've identified the two big purposes of data, there are two logistical questions left to consider.

How do we get and keep track of all of this data?

Data can only be a vital part of our work with students if it's easy to record, use, and retrieve. This doesn't always mean every data source has to be in the same location, but it does mean you need to think about how it's gathered, where it's stored, and how easy it is to access. Most counseling offices have data in three key places:

- The school's student information system. This resource usually gives counselors access to the key information needed to assess at-risk students (attendance, grades, discipline, family reports, etc.). Counselors may also use an area within the system to record notes of meetings with students and college-related information. As long as this area is password protected, making the most of it helps reduce the number of places data is stored.

- The counseling information system. Some schools have special programs just for counselor information. This can include notes from meetings with students, college test scores, and records of student applications to colleges and scholarship programs. This information is often used to produce annual reports on the entire counseling program. As long as college data can be easily extracted from other counseling data, this is a great place to keep college information—including reports colleges may send you on how your students are doing in their studies.

- External websites. Counselors may have access to websites where the state or federal government keeps track of your students or graduates. While these websites generally provide information on graduating classes as a whole—and they might use some of those data points counselors don't see as helpful in their work—it's important to be aware of these resources, since others may judge the value of your school (or your counseling program) on this information.

More counselors are finding it hard to access basic information on their students, such as attendance records, without having to request the information from an administrator. Since these requests can limit counselor efficacy with students, it's important to have a discussion with your principal on what data you need regular access to, and why you need it. Many administrators will give you your own account, glad that they don't have to process your many requests anymore, so be sure to ask for the data you need to help students.

Are you disaggregating the right way?

Average ACT scores for the senior class tell you how the group does as a whole, but how are the at-risk students performing on the test? Are there differences in the math scores based on gender? Do your scores tell you anything about ways your school needs to improve college readiness for students of color, or students whose first language is something other than English? Do the students from one of your feeder middle schools perform better on the science test and, if so, why? Are first-generation students going on to college at the same rate as other students?

College readiness is only one part of assessing a school's effectiveness, but many college measures can help school leaders update curriculum, school climate, and course offerings in important ways. Be sure to think about how you can break down data to make it meaningful for yourself and others. Just like all counseling, college counseling is most effective when we look past group trends, and determine the needs of individual students.

Notes and Follow-Up

- Revisit one of your data points—grades or college test scores—and see how easy it is to disaggregate the data by gender, feeder school, and free/reduced lunch status. If this is difficult to do, consider who you need to talk with to improve your access to disaggregated data.

- Data is a growing field in all of school counseling, but especially college counseling. Take a look at these two sources as ongoing supports for your effort to better use data:
  - *The Use of Data in High School Counseling: Hatching Results for Students, Programs, and the Profession** by Trish Hatch
  - *Higher Ed Data Stories*, a regular blog posted by Jon Boeckenstedt, associate vice president for enrollment management and marketing, DePaul University.

10

Chapter 4
WHAT'S A COLLEGE COUNSELING CURRICULUM?

Many people—including some school counselors—are surprised to discover there's more to a college counseling curriculum than applying to college and getting admitted. Just as an English teacher develops a curriculum designed to deliver the essential knowledge and skills of English, school counselors design a curriculum that helps every student (that's *every* student) understand the world of college and what it has to offer.

If done well, an effective college counseling curriculum offers students opportunities to engage in self-discovery, critical thinking, analysis, synthesis, research, team building, and effective communication skills. Far more than just completing an application and hoping for the best, a true college counseling curriculum gives students the chance to understand more about themselves and the world around them, and how to interact with the world—all while considering the question, "Is college for me?"

A strong college counseling curriculum has two parts. **College awareness** is an understanding of the college opportunities that exist and the skills and activities needed to get into a college and enroll (also called matriculation). **College readiness** addresses the knowledge, skills, habits, and activities a student will need to make the most of the college experience and achieve their college goals.

One of the challenges in building a college counseling curriculum is that both college awareness and college readiness need to be taught at the same time. Students who spend all of ninth and tenth grade learning about college options won't be college ready if they haven't learned the study skills, perseverance, and team-building activities the college experience requires. On the other hand, students with great grades and impressive extracurricular activities may sell themselves short if the first time they visit any college campus is the fall of twelfth grade.

Knowing when to teach which parts of both college awareness and college readiness is a mix of science and art. Data can help counselors know the college-going history of the families in their community, and that can help drive decisions about which parts to emphasize, and when. Students may need early exposure to four-year colleges if most parents attended community college or entered the workforce right after high school. At the same time, counselors may need to make an early introduction to the benefits of technical certificates or community college to students in a community where most parents hold a bachelor's degree.

These discussions may not be easy, but they're important. The high cost of college, combined with the challenges some college graduates are having in the job market, are leading many families to think twice about the value of college. Students (and parents) need to know early about the economic, vocational, and personal benefits of college, largely through classroom presentations and large group activities. Depending on the community, this introduction may need to start in elementary school. Whenever they start, the goal is to have every student take a close look at college as one of the many postsecondary options, and be ready to decide which college option, if any, is for them.

That doesn't mean college readiness lessons are wasted on students who don't choose college. Employers value most of the skills that make for successful college students; it's just that students will use them on the job site, rather than in the classroom. The cost of college also suggests some students will wait to go, entering the workforce first to save for college. In that case, the college readiness lessons counselors teach students as ninth or tenth graders will still come in handy once the student matriculates later in life.

Notes and Follow-Up

- Write a one-hundred-word summary of the college attitudes and expectations your parents and community have for the students you serve. Do they expect them to go to college? Why or why not? What kind of colleges do they see them attending, and why? What may be preventing them from thinking of a wider range of college options—including, for some communities, the option of not attending college?

- What data do you have to support the summary you've just written? Would data on parents' education level, community occupational trends, and local or statewide economic reports help you build your college counseling curriculum? If so, where can you access this information for your community and state?

Chapter 5
WHAT GOES INTO A COLLEGE COUNSELING CURRICULUM?

A college counseling curriculum is designed to address a few key questions:

- What will be taught?
- How will it be taught?
- When it will be taught?
- How will the teaching be measured?

These questions are best addressed by considering the qualities we want in our curriculum.

Qualities of a Strong College Counseling Curriculum

- It contains the essential components of what the student needs to know.
- It contains benchmarks outlining expected student achievement.
- It contains outcomes that are measurable.
- It contains components that are sequential.
- It contains components that are time specific.

- Each component offers flexible delivery methods allowing for individuality.

Keeping those in mind, each component of the College Counseling Curriculum should include the following:

- A goal. What is the skill/information/attitude the student will demonstrate upon completion of this component?
- Methods. What methods will be used to realize this goal?
- Materials. What materials will be needed to complete the method?
- Skills acquired. Even if the goal isn't a specific skill set, what skills will the student have to demonstrate in order to reach the goal?
- Assessment/Evaluation. How will the student's understanding be measured, and will this take place as learning is occurring (assessment) or at the end of the activity (evaluation)?
- Recordkeeping. How will the counselor and/or student keep track of this work for future reference, if at all?

Remembering that a college counseling curriculum has two tracks that are running at the same time (college readiness and college awareness), and these two tracks could be taught as early as elementary school, this is starting to sound like a lot of very serious work.

It's a good thing there are resources to help.

NACAC Step by Step will get you well on your way to developing a strong college awareness curriculum. Developed by the

National Association for College Admission Counseling, *Step by Step* has a rich history of success in introducing colleges and the college application process to a wide array of students, having particular success with students who come from low-income areas, or are the first in their family to attend college of any kind. The curriculum starts with middle school, but it can be adapted to younger or older grades, and includes presentations in English and Spanish—all for free.

NOSCA Eight Components comes from College Board's National Office for School Counselor Advocacy. Focusing on college awareness and college readiness, Eight Components offers a comprehensive scope-and-sequence approach to the content of a college counseling curriculum, with key considerations on how to use, generate, and share data. Eight Components nicely overlaps with many career counseling goals as well, and while it doesn't offer lesson-plan ready presentations, it helps you frame the big picture.

MCAN College Application Week is one of three curriculum-rich activities the Michigan College Access Network offers that can anchor a college counseling curriculum. *College Application Week* shows counselors how to hold a weeklong celebration of college every fall, where each senior applies to at least one college. *The College Cash Campaign* helps counselors engage all students to file for financial aid, while *College Decision Day* offers examples of how schools can celebrate the postsecondary plans of all students in a powerful way.

Successful implementation of these resources will give students and parents a clear look at all kinds of college options, and allow them to reflect on the options that make the most sense to them.

Notes and Follow-Up

- Spend ten minutes scanning through the *NOSCA Eight Components* unit focused on the grade level you work with. What one area of the college counseling curriculum could your school use to improve service to students?

- Spend fifteen minutes in the *Step by Step* curriculum. What one activity can you implement right away that will improve your college counseling curriculum?

- Spend five minutes looking at the *MCAN College Application Week* website. Which of their three programs would best advance your college counseling goals?

Chapter 6
COUNSELING ADVISORY COMMITTEES

It isn't unusual for counselors to feel a little overwhelmed at the idea of creating and implementing a K-12 college counseling curriculum all by themselves. This is a natural and important response, for three reasons:

1. You really can't do it by yourself.
2. Recognizing that means you won't actually try and do it all by yourself, which would be crazy.
3. Recognizing that increases the chances you'll ask others to help you.

Students looking for college help often have to build bridges with others. That's exactly what counselors need to do here. Given everything counselors do, and the scope of a full-blown college counseling curriculum, they need to be the leaders and coordinators of their schools' college counseling curriculum, but they cannot be the sole implementers.

All of these ideas come from real-life examples of **curricular collaboration**. This comes from a simple idea that often gets overlooked: if college counseling only occurs in the counseling office when the counselor is there, everyone is in trouble. That's why counselors need a **Counseling Advisory Committee (CAC).**

Developed by counseling guru Norm Gysbers, a CAC brings together every major group that has an interest in the success of the counseling department, giving counselors a chance to talk with them about department goals, what the department is doing, and what it should be doing. The group doesn't need to meet often (maybe two to three times a year), and the counselors coordinate the first few meetings.

In terms of CAC membership, consider who in the community either cares or should care about what counselors do and are willing to serve as their eyes and ears (and voice). That list usually includes the principal, the athletic director, a teacher or two, the PTA president, the leaders of the town's religious organizations, the president of the local chamber of commerce, the education writer on the local paper, the owner of the skateboard park where the kids hang out all summer, the owner of the local snack shop—you get the idea. CACs usually start at around twelve to fifteen members, with others added as new needs and opportunities arise for the counseling department.

The CAC has three main roles:

Communication advocates. A good counseling program is largely limited by the perceptions of that program by the community it serves, so counselors need to be in the information loop. Members agree they will actively keep counselors informed about the trends, concerns, and issues affecting the community in general, and students in particular, as well as the community's opinions about the school counseling program. They also agree to promote the goals of the counseling program and share information with others about upcoming counseling programs and activities.

Curriculum assistance. A promising engineering student needs help finding an internship. Counselors have developed a great college essay workshop, but need to find a teacher willing to present it. Parents aren't filing the FAFSA, and it's unclear why this is happening. CAC members help counselors make connections to sources and resources, as well as make sure the school's counseling curriculum doesn't overlap with services families can get from other local agencies.

Big picture thinkers. It shouldn't happen at every meeting, but CACs help anticipate the new needs and directions of the students and families you serve and support long-range planning.

It takes a village to raise a child, and most counselors have 450 children on their caseload. Let the village help you.

Notes and Follow-Up

- Draw up the list of individuals you would like to have on your Counseling Advisory Committee. Once you're finished, check it for balance. Does this represent the key voices of the student advocates in the school? Outside the school?

- Discuss the idea of a Counseling Advisory Committee with your principal. To prepare for that meeting, draw up a list of goals for the CAC, using the goals you have for your department as your guide. Be sure to include the list of members, and schedule the two to three dates the committee will meet—typically in the school, either during the school day or right after school.

Chapter 7
MAPPING AND NEWSLETTERS

It's important to share your college counseling curriculum with your Counseling Advisory Committee, since CAC members shape what the community expects of students in many areas, including college. It's also important to share your college counseling curriculum with students, because they are the beneficiaries of these lessons.

The third group that deserves clear communication of the college counseling curriculum is parents. Since every adult already has a preexisting opinion on the virtues of college, and how much good it will (or won't) do their child to attend, it's important to create structures that give parents a fresh look at the college selection process. Creating opportunities for parents to update their perceptions about college is one of the best ways a counselor can support a student's growth.

Two important ways counselors share their college counseling curriculum are through **mapping** and **newsletters**. Mapping provides parents with the big picture; it links the goals and qualities of the curriculum with the activities and events the student will complete. This is usually displayed in a chart or series of charts that depict the curricular elements of each grade. These charts are shared at the first parent program of every year, displayed in the counseling office, and always accessible on the counseling office website.

The second way to communicate the college counseling curriculum to parents is through regular newsletters. While mapping gives parents the scope and sequence of the curriculum, newsletters provide parents with information on how the curriculum is implemented, one step at a time. Reminders of due dates, upcoming events, and discussions of current trends in college admissions go into these newsletters, which are usually e-mailed to parents and archived on the counseling office website.

In terms of frequency, each newsletter has its own pace. College counseling newsletters for grades nine and ten are usually produced monthly. While students are actively engaged in college readiness activities in these grades, updates on study skills, extracurricular activities, and community service fit nicely into a newsletter that comes out eight or nine times in the school year.

Since the logistics of college awareness begin to increase in eleventh grade, the junior newsletter comes out more often. Typically, an edition will come out every other week in the first half of the junior year, then weekly in the second half of the year. Each newsletter may not bring completely new information, but given the multitude of logistical college tasks juniors need to complete, reminders of previously published deadlines and events are usually welcome.

The senior year newsletter mirrors the eleventh grade newsletter, with the twelfth grade edition coming out weekly in the first half of the senior year, and every other week in the second half.

This reflects the need for seniors to be more aware of application deadlines and activities in the fall.

If all of this newsletter publication work sounds time consuming, it is—for the first year. Counselors who digitally archive newsletters typically find the important events for a particular grade come up at the same time of the school year, every year. As a result, it isn't unusual for a counselor to pull up the senior newsletter from the previous year in the second week of October and review it, modify a due date or two, and send it out to the current year's seniors at the same time. Since the audience for each newsletter is new every year, innovative content is less of an issue. The greater issue is timely content, and that rarely changes.

Notes and Follow-Up

- Many states have a *Comprehensive School Counseling Model* that emulates or at least includes the comprehensive school counseling model of the American School Counseling Association. Since many of these models have a template for mapping a counseling curriculum, find your state counseling model, and see what tools it offers you.

- Spend twenty minutes writing a one-page back-to-school newsletter for high school seniors. What key points would you address, knowing they would be getting another newsletter the following week? Don't worry about format; just focus on content, limit yourself to one page, and create a newsletter file in your computer.

- Counselors should also send a copy of every newsletter to their principal, faculty, and grade-level parents. Consider how you might do this through websites, e-mail, or both.

Chapter 8
WEBSITES AND COLLEGE HANDBOOKS

When it comes to communicating the college counseling program in a comprehensive way, these are hard times for counselors. Some parents want everything on paper, while others want everything online—and if there is both a print version and an online version, they'd better say the same thing, requiring twice as much updating.

One solution is to create a college handbook as a PDF, and post it on the counseling website. Families who want everything on paper can print the PDF (or request the college counseling office to do so). Families who want everything online can read the handbook from the website—and since PDFs can include web links, online users can directly click to sites referenced in the PDF.

With this approach, counselors only have to make and maintain one version of the handbook, but, like all simple solutions, there are challenges. Print parents may not have access to printers, and the counseling office may not have the budget to print copies for everyone, while online parents may say this isn't *really* online, since the content is just a wordy document posted on a website.

The other major issue is how to present the information—as individual college handbooks for each grade, or as one massive handbook given to each student? Again, there's no clear path here; any changes to the "one size fits all" book means every student has to get a new copy of the handbook every year, while grade-by-grade books may leave parents with questions about what's next.

The best way to solve this problem is to write as if you were going to create separate handbooks and then see what each one looks like. If the ninth and tenth grade editions look skinny all by themselves, consider combining them into one. In many cases, one combined edition also works for grades eleven and twelve.

If you decide to go with one book, be ready for repetition. Most high schools will have sections for each grade, then include the same information again by subject—so all the testing information would be combined, all the college visit information, and so on. If there is separate copy online, that's up to four places that have overlapping information, and suddenly, the counselor's IT work is getting out of hand.

In terms of content, everything goes in—everything: philosophy, goals, mappings, month-by-month calendar, the three parts of the college readiness curriculum and why they matter, summer programs, the different kinds of college visits, testing, applying, letters of recommendation, scholarship information, and that's just the start. As a rule, if it's mentioned in this book, it's in the handbook. The counselor strategy discussions aren't included, but almost all other topics need some kind of coverage.

No matter how the handbook is shared, consider the user-friendliness of the counseling website. Just putting a PDF on the site doesn't make it that attractive or welcoming, so be sure to include lists—test dates, test prep, scholarship websites, summer program websites, community service programs, links to college search engines—that all need to stay fresh.

Some people look at high school counseling websites and see nothing but old information, usually because counselors choose people over product when time is short, and time is always short. This makes it vital to find a way to keep the site current, even if someone else ends up doing it.

Notes and Follow-Up

- This is likely one of the first issues you should discuss with your Counseling Advisory Committee. There are commercial printers and programmers in the community who could make your handbook and web challenges go away overnight. Just make sure your school's IT team is represented, in case a CAC member volunteers to create your web pages or pay for print copies. Some schools have rules about who may and may not create content.

- Look at your current college counseling handbook. What do you like about it? What could be improved? How is it different from the college counseling handbook for the three high schools closest to you—or three random high schools you look at online when doing a *high school college counseling handbook* website search?

Chapter 9
SUPPORT FROM YOUR PRINCIPAL

The principal is part of the Counseling Advisory Committee, even if the counselor's direct supervisor is another administrator. There are two main reasons for this:

- The principal is seen as the leader of the building. If counseling matters to the principal, it matters to everyone in the building.

- The principal is the procurer of budgets, clerical help, facilities, and fellow counselors, all essential elements of a strong counseling program.

It isn't uncommon to hear stories from veteran counselors whose program was changed for better or worse when a new principal took over their school. The number of school counseling programs that can thrive over time with an indifferent principal is remarkably small. Winning them over, and keeping them close, is a must.

Fortunately, resources exist to achieve three important goals to win an administrator's support.

Agree on the duties counselors do and don't have. Counselors often swear their job description is being made up as the school year goes along, and depends on which teachers are absent that day, or how bad the weather is. Every educator needs to be flexible, but if math teachers can be confident they'll be teaching math every day, aren't counselors entitled to the same assurance?

That's where the Annual Agreement comes in. Designed by the American School Counselor Association, the *Annual Agreement (Annual Agreement ASCA National Model)* is a document completed by a school counselor and their principal that outlines the counselor's duties every year. From outlining the hours the counseling office will be open to allocating percentages of time to various duties, this agreement gives principals and counselors a chance to create an overview of the counselor's role in the school that's based on planning, and not reaction.

Ask about the administrator's counseling goals. By asking the principal to outline their goals for the school counseling program, the counselor understands which parts of the program are valued, and which may be misunderstood. Once the principal's goals are clear, data can be used to show them how well those counseling components are or aren't working, leading to a discussion of how those results could be even better.

NOSCA's Principal-Counselor Relationship publication offers resources and research on how to create a common set of goals and a strong working relationship. This can get an administrator's attention and support in ways agreements and surveys often can't, and it makes counseling challenges more real to them.

Explore the administrative support counselors need. It helps if administrators see the big picture of what counselors do; it helps even more when administrators offer support that advances the work counselors do. I did some research in 2000 that uncovered five key areas where counselors want administrative support for their work, and a tool exists to measure those areas. Twenty-nine questions offer counselors a better understanding of the support an administrator is giving and how counselors can get more support in the areas where it's needed. The questionnaire is grounded in the research-based premise that the quality of the administrator's support can be accurately measured by the counselor's recognition of that support. In other words, if counselors feel their administrators are offering support, they are; if not, there's room for growth.

The questionnaire is in the back of the book. It's copyrighted, but it's fine to make one copy for you to complete, and a second one for your administrator to complete. Comparing answers can be a great way to jumpstart a conversation about the support an administrator is providing, and how it could improve.

Notes and Follow-Up

- Take a look at either the *ASCA Annual Agreement* or *NOSCA's Principal-Counselor Relationship*. How might one of these tools help you create a stronger relationship with your principal?

- Copy and complete the administrative support questionnaire in the back of this book. Where are you receiving the most support from your principal? Where are you receiving the least—and how can you get more?

Chapter 10
CLOSING ACHIEVEMENT GAPS

Community involvement and administrative leadership are essential elements of the college counseling curriculum for all students, but there are three groups in particular that will need the full support of the school and the community in investigating college options, and preparing for life after high school, no matter where life may take them.

The first group is made up of students whose abilities and talents are greater than their grades and achievements would suggest. This can include:

- The student who knows the answer to every math problem written on the board but earns low grades because she doesn't turn in her homework.

- The student who writes brilliant essays, but never participates in class.

- The student with the magnificent voice who sings in the hallways between classes, but doesn't join choir.

- The straight-A student whose life interests are a perfect fit for a highly selective four-year college, but whose family insists she attend community college.

- The student who has that special something you can't quite describe, but gets by with Cs and Ds.

Most students who demonstrate an achievement gap have a story to tell, and in most cases, it's unique—so it isn't likely that story will be understood through their participation in a group counseling activity. Individualizing the college counseling experience is a must for these students, and since a counselor's time is in short supply, the rest of the community has to pitch in. This can be done by taking these measures:

Data analysis. Students need to articulate their stories, but the achievement gaps of some students may have a common root. Historically, some of these roots lie in gender (fewer women going into math, science, and tech careers), income (low-income students not pursuing college, or not pursuing a demanding college), ethnicity (students of color not pursuing or completing college at the same rate as their peers) or the first in the family to go to college (not completing college).

All educators want to take every precaution not to pigeon-hole any student, but a data analysis of underachieving and high-absenteeism students can often provide some clues to the obstacles those students face that can be overcome. Start there, and be ready to individualize.

Observation and discussion. The local minister may know the bright math student babysits younger siblings, and doesn't have time to do homework; a veteran teacher may see a pattern of behavior in a younger sibling that was present in their older sibling, and share how it was overcome; a community business leader may be able to explain why the parent of a bright child doesn't want them to go away to college. A well-trained College Advisory Committee can work confidentially with key leaders in the school to share insights on low-achieving students that can serve as the basis for a plan of support.

Building and implementing interventions. Programs including community-based study halls, after-school child care for siblings, and parent-to-parent college support groups can be created to meet the needs of low-achieving students. Utilizing all of the school and community resources means school counselors don't have to oversee or implement all of these interventions—and that's good. This means students will receive messages of affirmation and possibility from many adults, a key component to gaining self-esteem and realizing more of their goals.

Assessment and modification. Outcomes of these programs should be recorded and discussed, so successful programs can be strengthened and less successful plans can be modified. This closes the loop of intervention; more importantly, it gives students the clear message that they matter.

Notes and Follow-Up

- Since you know how to disaggregate your data from your work with chapter 3, select two data points and see if the disaggregated data relates to college attainment. Your goal is to determine what's getting in the way of students realizing greater success.

- If you find a relationship, develop a list of intervention strategies that could close this achievement gap. List the key people, resources, and materials that would be needed, and be sure to consider how you will evaluate the intervention for success and modification.

Chapter 11
MIDDLE SCHOOL COLLEGE COUNSELING

Every school counselor has to consider the needs and interests of their community when building a college counseling curriculum, and that is especially true in middle school, our second group that requires special community attention. Research shows that a good amount of introductory college counseling has to occur in middle schools that work with low-income students and students who will be the first in their family to go to college. That same approach will be a disaster in a community where nearly every parent has gone to college; one too many sixth grade parent program about the benefits of college, and counselors could be overwhelmed with requests to start middle school test prep and college essay seminars.

Knowing what's at stake for too much (or too little) college counseling at the middle school level, it's important to keep the big picture in mind. Middle school is where many kids get turned off to school. The additional peer pressures and identity issues that come with adolescence lead many students to decide it isn't "cool" to shine in the classroom. This is especially true with girls in the math and science fields, but it can happen with boys as well. When these doubts lead to weak schedule choices in classes, students come to high school lacking the rigor they need (again, especially in math) to get to the high-level courses they need to make the most of their talents, and to be college ready. The middle school college counseling curriculum must address those issues, and create healthier messages for students to build on.

That's why it's important to give the right kind of college message. College counseling researcher Patricia McDonough talks about the **predisposition phase of college counseling**, where students gain a greater awareness about the purposes of college, the kinds of colleges that exist, the requirements for college admission, and the ways families can pay for college. Students shouldn't use this phase to develop a list of colleges they want to apply to. The goals of this phase are more general, such as an appreciation of the difference between a large research university, a small residential liberal arts college, and a community college.

This is where the college counseling curriculum and the needs of middle schoolers blend so nicely. By exposing middle school students to college requirements, students will begin to make a connection between the grades they are earning now and the options they'll have later—a perfect place for study skills to jump in and fill any potential void. By showing students in grades six through eight that colleges are places to meet new people, go to great football games *and* study, colleges become models for a balance of academic and social behaviors. By organizing field trips for families to nearby college campuses on a weekend, counselors allow parents and students to explore college together and separately at the same time, taking family communications to a new level.

There is likely to be some overlap between the ninth grade college counseling curriculum and the ideas shared with middle schoolers, and that is more than fine. Many students start high school in a new building, and that makes it the perfect time to remind them that, while some things have changed, some things haven't—like the benefits of study skills, extracurriculars, and community service.

Notes and Follow-Up

- Read and review the college counseling curriculum in your middle school. What are its strengths? What are its weaknesses? How well does it connect to the college counseling curriculum in the high school? How often do middle school counselors and high school counselors discuss their college counseling programs?

- Take a look at the NACAC Middle School Curriculum, and identify two activities that would be appropriate to use in your community.

Chapter 12
NINTH GRADE COLLEGE COUNSELING

It's been said that every student wants to go to Harvard on at least two days of their life: the first day of ninth grade, and the first day of twelfth grade. Their ability to actually go there, the saying continues, depends on what they do with the thousand days in between.

This is why the third key group where community- and school-based resources come into play with college counseling is in ninth grade—specifically, in the area of college readiness. It's certainly important to talk with ninth graders about different college options. But if students hear too much about the magical experience of college, without knowing how to get there, it becomes too easy for students to think going to college is something they simply have to wish for, and it comes true. Even high-achieving students need to know that isn't the case, especially if they're applying to colleges in high demand.

That's where college readiness comes in. The more that students demonstrate the qualities colleges are looking for, the more college options they'll be keeping open throughout their high school career. To do that, a strong college counseling curriculum shows ninth graders the importance of college readiness in three key areas:

Being a good student. Most students know good grades are a key part of a successful college application, but they don't always know there's more to it than that. Colleges also consider students' strength of schedule: how challenging were the classes they took, and did they have the opportunity to take more demanding classes? In addition, many colleges ask for letters of recommendation and student essays to get beyond grades, to see if the students were actively engaged in their learning and what they now know about themselves and the world as a result of all of this schooling.

This level of understanding requires much more than good grades; it requires that students learn how to learn. With the leadership of their principal, teachers should incorporate study skill lessons into their teaching, and make sure that assignments require key elements such as doing research, writing rough drafts, thinking critically, and pursuing meaningful independent study. Every student has their own successful approach to studying, and teachers can help students in their discovery and utilization of that approach.

Involvement in extracurricular activities. Colleges know learning occurs outside the classroom; that's why they want to know how the student spends their time once the school day is done. While some colleges like to see many of their applicants involved in athletics, there's no magic mixture of clubs and sports that guarantees admission to every applicant at any college.

This means students are wise to follow their interests when it comes to extracurriculars, and that usually means showing depth of commitment in a few things, rather than surface involvement in many. Since different students are interested in different things, schools and communities should work together to make sure a wide array of activities are available. Programs like robotics, 4H, and Boys and Girls Clubs are natural extra-curriculars to include.

Ninth grade is also the time to show students how to record all of their activities and achievements, so they will have a complete record to use when applying to college. Programs like *Naviance** have a space for students to keep track of what they've done, while other students will use a spreadsheet, or a notebook. There's no one best way for all students to do this; counselors just need to make sure each student is getting it done.

Notes and Follow-Up

- Every school approaches study skills differently. Identify the teachers in your school who are focused and/or successful with teaching study skills. What do they do that makes a difference for their students? How can the Counseling Advisory Committee support expanding these efforts to include all students in all classes?

- Review the list of extracurricular activities in your school and community. What activities need to be added? Which need to be retired? Do students have easy access to this list (which includes contact information for the leader of each activity) on the school and counseling website?

- What resources does the school offer students for record-ing their extracurricular activities? Are students using it? How could it be better promoted?

Chapter 13
COMMUNITY SERVICE AND JOBS

The third area of college readiness in a ninth grade college counseling curriculum is student engagement in community service. From running the local soup kitchen to preparing for the annual Memorial Day parade, community service experiences give students the opportunity to develop skills of giving back and reaching out to others that will benefit them for a lifetime, and keep essential components of communities running at full capacity.

Community service is a key component to student development and college readiness, but there are two misconceptions that need to be cleared up. First, just like participation in a sport is not a guarantee of college admission, students participating in community service don't automatically gain an advantage in the application process at most colleges. Colleges that have a mission focused on service will certainly see voluntary community service as a vital part of a student's application, but most colleges view community service as one of many extracurricular activities students can engage in to learn more about themselves and the world around them.

This is especially true if the student is reporting community service hours they had to complete to graduate from high school. Mandatory community service is often seen as an important way high schools help students understand more about their relationship to their hometown, and colleges respect that goal. At the same time, most colleges don't consider fulfillment of a graduation requirement as volunteerism, since the student isn't choosing to do the work. Students should still list these hours on a college application, but since the school profile will explain the high school's community service requirement, the effect of this work will likely be muted.

Second, students need to know that colleges don't have a preferred kind of community service. Colleges certainly see the value of volunteering forty hours at the local homeless shelter, but they'll give equal value to a student volunteering forty hours coaching basketball at the local gym, or giving forty hours teaching students how to knit. Students can follow their passions with community service, making their contributions more of a true gift of their time and talents.

There's also flexibility in terms of how the service is given. One to two hours of tutoring each school week is just as impressive as offering the same number of total hours to a camp as a volunteer for a month in the summer. Like other extracurricular activities, commitment to one service project over many years and involvement in leadership opportunities offer extra weight to the experience for both the student and the college application. What students do and when they are offered are up to the students.

Finally, it's important to note that colleges also place value on the life lessons students learn if they choose to work, or, more importantly, have to work, instead of engaging in extracurriculars or community service. Colleges recognize the discipline, teamwork, and initiative required for students to balance school and work commitments. This is especially true if the student has to work to help support their family, a point that should be brought to the college's attention in the counselor's letter of recommendation. Not every college application has a separate section for work experience, but jobs can be listed in the activities section.

Ninth graders often start high school with big plans for attending a dream college. With the right school and community support, a college readiness curriculum that focuses on the pursuit of learning, exploration of extracurricular activities, and appropriate community service, can show all freshmen how to make that dream come true.

Notes and Follow-Up

- Check how the school collects information on community service and job opportunities, and how that information is shared with students and parents. This can appear on the same counseling website as extracurricular activities.

- Contact the members of your Counseling Advisory Committee, or discuss community service and student employment at your next CAC meeting. Community members can be a rich source of contacts and information for community service activities and jobs.

- There is a feeling among many counselors that the best way to instill the community service habit with ninth graders is to have them engage in volunteer work with their families. Check your list of community service activities, see how many family-friendly activities you have, and consider sources that can offer additional family opportunities.

Chapter 14
SUMMER PROGRAMS

Where summer programs used to be limited to credit recovery activities run out of the local school district, summer enrichment programs of all kinds are now being offered by high schools, colleges, and private companies around the world, opening students to all kinds of supplemental learning experiences.

High-achieving students are interested in participating in these programs for many reasons, and they often turn to counselors to explore the programs that are best for them. In addition to keeping up with the latest summer offerings, counselors will want to keep these points in mind when talking with students about their summer plans, especially as they relate to the college counseling curriculum:

New learning opportunities. Summer programs should always be seen as a chance to learn something new, usually with new people, and often in a new place. These programs are attractive to many students because they bring together committed learners who like the subject matter at hand—something that doesn't always happen when students are taking mandatory classes at their local school.

Benefit to college applications. As students sort through their summer options, they'll often think about taking a particular program because they think it will "look good to colleges." It's certainly true that colleges like to see students engaged in learning outside the classroom, but there's no single summer program that will improve a student's chances of admission at any college, or every college, and there's no need to participate in one (or more) every single summer. Students are wise to follow their interests when selecting a summer program.

Summer programs at their dream school. This is especially true of summer programs offered on the campus of the student's first-choice college. Attending that program usually has little effect on a student's chances of admission there. Many summer programs are run by a private company that rents space on the college campus. It may appear the program is related to the college, but that's not always the case, and if it is, the admissions office may be unaware of the program's existence.

Programs related to the student's major. There's something to be said for pre-med students who participate in a summer medical program, or journalism majors who attend an intensive writing workshop. At the same time, there can be great benefit for the pre-law student to spend the summer reading literature, or learning more about geology. Some highly selective programs (like accelerated medical programs) may see related summer experiences as a plus, but others will appreciate students who branch out and try something new.

Summer community service trips. Busy students often use their summer break to participate in community service activities they don't have time for during the school year, but this doesn't always mean they have to travel overseas to do so. Colleges certainly see the value in missionary work and global assistance, but as a rule, most would rather see a long-term commitment to a local community service project than brief, non-missionary service in a distant location that offers no chance for follow-up once the student is home.

Summer work still works. The increase in summer opportunities shouldn't discourage students from seeking out summer employment in their hometown, or internships and job-shadowing opportunities a student creates on their own. There's much to be said for taking the initiative to create one's own summer experience, and colleges value the many skills students can pick up in a summer job—especially if it's part of a work commitment that lasts several summers.

Notes and Follow-Up

- *College Express Summer Program Search* has a rich list of summer programs for students to investigate. Review this list for programs offered at the colleges near your high school. If they are missing from your list of summer programs, be sure to add them.
- Make a note to ask the admissions representatives from each college that visits your high school about the summer programs their school offers.
- Unlike other community service or extracurricular activities, families are likely to need advice on when and how to apply for these programs. Be sure to include this information when displaying the list and links for summer programs on your counseling website.
- Many students are likely to need financial support to participate in some of these programs. Work with your

Counseling Advisory Committee to develop a list of potential resources; Midwest high schools should see if their female students could qualify for financial assistance from the *Joyce Ivy Foundation*.

- School profiles have been mentioned twice, so it may be time to look at an example. A *high school profile* search should get you to some helpful examples by College Board, as well as some real-life examples from other high schools. Compare three to your current profile, and make a list of what to change.

Chapter 15
TENTH GRADE AND COLLEGE VISITS

Students will spend all of their high school years adding to their toolbox of study skills, increasing the depth and breadth of their extracurricular experiences, and learning more about the value of the give-and-take experience community service and work offer in a way nothing else can. With the right support, opportunities, and advice from the counseling office, the school, and the community, students will have the right mix of challenge, support, and opportunity in these three key areas, making for a secondary school experience of incredible growth.

As students grow, the college counseling curriculum grows with them. Building on the basic understandings developed about college in middle school, college awareness activities play a larger role in tenth grade after being somewhat dormant in ninth grade. Activities will vary from community to community, but the college counseling program for most tenth graders needs to focus on two areas in particular: college visits, and testing.

Tenth grade may seem a little early for students to tour colleges, but if done the right way, sophomores will return from these visits with a new understanding of the purpose of both high school and college. High schools are filled with all kinds of conversations about college; imagine the energy and meaning students can give to their high school experience once they see a college for themselves. Like the inspiration a budding musician gets from attending a concert, students will find a greater purpose to the work they're doing as sophomores, since they now see it as steps toward a bigger goal.

A good first activity is a college night for tenth graders in January. Admissions representatives from local colleges want to spend most of the fall focusing on seniors, but many of them will find time in the winter to talk to sophomores and their parents about the college experience. These college nights usually have a panel presentation, where reps can emphasize the importance of everything counselors have talked to students about—grades, strength of schedule, extracurriculars, and community service. College reps may also talk about the special qualities, programs and offerings your students might want to see for themselves when they visit campus. Complete the program with a Q and A, and the evening is complete.

With that experience under their belts, tenth graders are ready for a campus visit. They should plan on taking the campus tour. It's certainly true that the guides who lead these tours are highly trained, and they are only showing the parts of the campus the college wants students to see—but these are the parts the college sees as most important. If a student takes the tour and is unimpressed, that likely means the college may not be what they are looking for.

Students should also try and tailor the visit to see anything they are interested in. If the sophomore has a major in mind, sitting in on a class is a great idea; if there isn't time for that, it can wait for junior year college visits. If students want to look at a dorm room or want to see the science labs, they usually can; they should call ahead of time to ask what their options are.

The goal in looking at local colleges is for students to see the different qualities at different colleges. If students leave tenth grade knowing every college has pizza parlors and bookstores that offer cool clothing, they'll have a better understanding of what makes colleges different when they start their eleventh grade college visits.

Notes and Follow-Up

- Develop a plan for a tenth grade college night. What two or three colleges would you invite to talk with your sophomores about college, and why? When might it be held so it won't interfere with winter sports or other special school activities? Given your community's expectations, what would be the desired outcomes for a tenth grade college night, and how would you measure those outcomes? To ease your planning, are there neighboring high schools that would be interested in offering a joint tenth grade college night?

- Develop a list of all colleges—two-year and four-year, public and private—that are a two-hour drive or less from your high school. Find out how students sign up for a campus tour, and then share that information with your tenth graders.

- Despite your intuitions, it's best *not* to arrange a whole class tour of a college campus. Tenth graders are likely to get much more out of the tour, and learn something about their role in college selection, if they make their own arrangements to tour a college. To support this autonomy, call your local colleges to find out the campus visit options they offer to younger students.

Chapter 16
TESTING, PART I

Deciding what preparatory college tests to offer tenth graders depends on the testing they've had in previous grades and the test scores that will help them most in the admissions process. This is one of the reasons why "it depends" is seen to be the best way to start the answer to most questions about the college admissions process, but we'll try to avoid that answer here.

Which test do colleges prefer? Midwest colleges used to take only the ACT; East and West Coast colleges used to take only the SAT. No more. There are stories here and there that some colleges prefer one over the other, but these stories relate to a thin handful of schools. It's always good to ask, but the answer will overwhelmingly be that colleges recruiting nationally will take either one or both.

Will colleges want to see the results of a tenth grade test? Since nearly all colleges requiring tests will take either one, the primary goal of choosing a tenth grade test is to make sure it prepares students for the test they'll take as juniors. Colleges don't ask to see PSAT 10 or Aspire scores, and high schools would do well to make sure these scores aren't posted on transcripts sent to colleges. The whole idea behind these tests is practice; they give the student a feel for the kinds of questions that will be asked on the SAT or ACT, the order of the questions on the test, and the time limits of each section. The results may have some effect on the school's curriculum, but that is secondary. The task at hand is preparing students for junior year college testing.

What does each test expect students to know? The answer to this question is in flux, as College Board is introducing a newly formatted SAT. Early descriptions and sample tests seem to suggest to some counselors that the SAT and ACT will cover the same content, with the reading sections of both tests addressing issues in science and social studies, as well as English. Some students with an interest in science may still want to take the ACT, since it has a separate science-reasoning section, but it's unclear if colleges will see that as a plus for a student who wants to major in science.

Should students consider taking both the ACT and the SAT? Many counselors have long said the only real way a student knows which test they'll do best on is to take both the SAT and ACT once and then take the test they're most comfortable with a second time. The changes to the SAT may lead counselors to alter that advice, if the format and content of the two tests end up being similar—and many counselors are expecting that to be the case. For now, since the content and flow of the new SAT aren't tried and true, many counselors are still advising students to take both, in case their personal test-taking style leads to a better score in one test.

But can't students use the predictive scores of Aspire and PSAT to determine the best test to take? Not really. Many students end up scoring much higher on the ACT or SAT than they do on the prep tests. While it's hard to say why, it does support the idea that students who want to get their best test result will want to take both.

Notes and Follow-Up

- *Understanding your ACT Aspire Results* and *PSAT 10* introduce the two college preparatory tests taken by many sophomores. Take a look at each one, and consider these questions:
    - What does each one test?
    - How long does it take to administer each test?
    - What does each test cost?
    - How are test results and reports disaggregated to students? To counselors?
    - How does each test relate to the current testing the district uses in other grades?

Chapter 17
TESTING, PART II

With some basic testing questions addressed, it's now time to consider the logistics of testing.

Should we offer both the Aspire and PSAT 10 to tenth graders? Some schools that use Aspire in lower grades will also offer the PSAT 10, since that prepares students for the eleventh grade PSAT, which determines initial eligibility for National Merit Scholarships. Other schools start offering Aspire in tenth or eleventh grade, but since the paper version of Aspire costs much more than the online version, cost is a factor, as is available technology.

What about cost? And time? In states that pay for all public school students to take the ACT in eleventh grade, it's probably wise to offer Aspire as the tenth grade test. For states that offer a free SAT, the PSAT is a wise choice. Offering both will help prepare students for the ACT and SAT, but two tests can take more time away from the school day, and it will take more time away from counseling duties, if the counselor doubles as the testing coordinator.

Are fee waivers available? College Board does offer fee waivers for the PSAT and the SAT, but not the PSAT 10. ACT offers fee waivers for the ACT, but not for any level of Aspire. Schools can consider offering the PSAT 10 and Aspire to low-income students at a reduced price, but that is up to school policy.

What about the relationship to our K-12 testing philosophy? Some districts will see the PSAT 10 and Aspire as natural extensions of the school-wide or district-wide testing done to measure student progress, while other districts will see this as a "stand-alone" testing experience only for college-bound students. You'll want to work with your principal to develop a rationale that makes the most sense for the students you serve, and then communicate that rationale clearly and frequently. Be sure to include an explanation of how prior testing prepares students for college admission testing. If it doesn't, it's better to explain why it doesn't than pretend it does.

What about sharing the results of the testing? Tenth grade college testing helps no one if there isn't time for students to consider what they need to do to be well prepared for future college tests. *College Board (Sharing PSAT 10 Results)* and *ACT (Understanding Your ACT Aspire Results)* offer help on how to share results with students. Counselors can use this information and develop small group workshops to share testing results with students, if high caseloads make it impossible to discuss test results individually. The time needed to share results is another factor to consider when deciding to offer one or two tests in tenth grade.

It's also important to consider how these results will be shared with parents, teachers, and the general community. Each of these audiences will do different things with the data you give them, and that may require you to disaggregate the data differently for each audience.

The College Advisory Committee can be invaluable in sharing this data with the community. The relationships the counselors have with committee members, combined with giving members an advance review of the results, can go a long way to shape the community's response to the results.

What about test prep? Some schools will use the sample questions the test makers provide to give students a sense of what to expect on the test. This can be done in the classroom, or in a special workshop. Private companies also offer test prep for these exams. Since colleges don't see the results of tenth grade tests, it may be wise to discourage extensive test prep and get a clear picture of where the students' performance naturally lies.

Notes and Follow-Up

- Review the answers you've developed for the Notes and Follow-Up section of chapter 16 and consider these additional points:
  - Do we have the technology and testing space required to offer both tests?
  - Will the fee waiver policy for either test adversely affect some students in my school?
  - How will I share the test results with students?
  - Is test prep needed for the tenth graders in my school?
  - How will I communicate this information to parents?

Chapter 18
ELEVENTH GRADE, AND "IT DEPENDS"

The eleventh grade college counseling curriculum builds on the strong foundation laid in grades nine and ten. The three main areas of college readiness continue to expand as students take on more challenging classes, and begin to assume leadership roles in extracurricular activities.

Two college readiness questions often come up at the start of eleventh grade. Student growth and expanded course offerings lead many juniors to wonder if they are better off to get a high grade in a regular section of a class, or take an honors (or advanced) section of a class and risk a lower grade.

The real answer to this question is another question: "Where will the student learn the most?" But there's a good chance students are asking because they want to know how their choice will affect their chances of admission at the colleges they're interested in—and that depends.

If a college uses the grade point average (GPA) the high school provides on the transcript, students' chances of admission can go down if they earn lower grades. Students applying to these colleges may decide to take less challenging classes, but if the college also looks at strength of schedule, the students may lose in degree of challenge what they gained in the higher grade.

If a college recomputes the student's GPA, it will likely give the student more points for earning higher grades in more demanding classes. While the amount of weight each college gives to advanced classes varies, it's generally true that the student will be better off taking the more demanding class, as long as they earn a B or higher. Earning anything lower than a B may cancel out any advantage the student has in taking the more demanding class, and in some cases, this low grade can hurt the student's chances of admission.

Students will also want to consider the effect a demanding class will have on the rest of their schedule. The study time needed to do well in Advanced Math, for example, may take away from the time needed to keep up with their other classes. If that's the case, the good grade in the advanced class doesn't outweigh the lower grades earned in the other classes.

Since different colleges handle more demanding classes in different ways, this is the first of many questions where the answer is "it depends." As a rule, however, students who are unsure they can earn a B in an advanced course without significant additional study time should carefully consider their choice.

The second question students commonly ask in eleventh grade is whether they can quit an extracurricular activity, or change their community service focus. This sometimes happens because students want to devote more time to their academics; other times students want to pursue something new.

Colleges would rather see depth of commitment in a few activities than shallow commitment in several—but they also don't want students to be unhappy. If the student wants to move on to a new activity, eleventh grade is a good time to do that; twelfth grade, less so.

Dropping all activities to focus on studies can raise concerns with colleges who look for something more than just good grades in strong classes. Then again, some students need more time with challenging classes to get the good grades these same colleges expect. Working with students to maintain a healthy balance of both is the goal, and depends on the interests of the colleges they're considering. Dropping one extracurricular is usually just fine; dropping more than that would require a thoughtful conversation.

Notes and Follow-Up

- Make a list of the five colleges that receive the most applications from your students, and write a summary of the GPA policy of each one. Do they take the GPA given on the transcript, or do they recompute GPA? If they recompute, which classes get extra weight? Honors classes? AP classes? IB classes? Do some receive more weight than others?

- If any summary seems incomplete, look up these policies on the college's website—or better yet, contact the college. This will be good information to have on hand, and to use for your college nights.

Chapter 19
ELEVENTH AND TWELFTH GRADE COLLEGE VISITS

Tenth graders visit the campuses of local colleges in order to get a feel for what college is all about, and how colleges are different. The idea of the visit is for them to see a few colleges first-hand, and begin to think about what they're looking for in their next school.

This goal changes in eleventh and twelfth grade, when students visit college campuses to see if a school is a good fit for them. Just like a tenth grade visit, juniors should plan on taking the campus tour, but they should also go with a list of questions written ahead of time that address what they want in a college experience. This certainly can include questions about major, class size, and study abroad, but it can also include questions about social life, residence halls, what the nearby town is like, and more. Whatever is of interest to the student is fair game.

The eleventh grade visits should also leave more time to explore each campus. In the interest of time, students and parents will often want to see several colleges on one trip. Students tell me the key to a good tour is to do absolutely no more than two colleges a day, and if the two colleges are more than an hour apart, students should really do them one day at a time. It's tempting to try and make more visits in fewer days, but even the best student's impression of four colleges can overlap if there is no breathing space between visits.

That cannot be emphasized enough. A parent told me she had her son spend a good amount of time at each college sitting in the middle of campus, watching people go by. This is a great way to take in the campus atmosphere while listening to what students have to say, adding a strong dimension to the visit.

Another good approach is for visiting students to simply ask college students a few simple questions—why did you choose this college, where else did you look, what's it like to go to school here, if you had it to do all over again, etc. High school students may be afraid they'll look like greenhorns if they ask these questions, but most college students are happy to oblige and incredibly honest with their answers.

The best time to visit a campus is when classes are in full swing, usually October, November, or February. Students often want to do eleventh grade visits during the summer, since vacation plans will take them to that part of the country, or their busy schedules won't let them visit during the school year. Students should tour the campus in summer by all means, as long as they go back to visit campus again after they're admitted. There is almost no circumstance where students should enroll at a college where they haven't sat in on at least one class.

Campus trips are also organized by private companies, youth groups, and sometimes by the colleges themselves. Again, these can be great tools, but students should look at the agenda, and count the colleges on each day's itinerary; if there are more than two, students are paying a lot of money just to get confused.

Students should record their impressions of each college *right after they leave campus* and before they discuss the visit with anyone—especially their parents. Comparing notes makes sense, but only after the student makes notes of their own.

Notes and Follow-Up

- Many high schools arrange staff professional development days or parent-teacher conferences to create three- and four-day weekends for students to visit college campuses. Look at your school calendar. What changes can be made to make it easier for students to visit distant colleges in the fall or winter?

- Review your school's policy for absences related to college visits. Are they excused? Unexcused? Do they have to be arranged in advance? Is there a limit all students must follow? How are students and parents notified of this policy?

- Write a one-hundred-word summary of the differences between taking a campus tour (on a regular school day) and attending a campus open house (where special programs and presentations occur). What are the plusses and minuses of each? Once it's finished, drop it in your newsletter file.

Chapter 20
COLLEGE FAIRS

A great way for students to take a first look at a college is to speak with an admissions officer at a college fair. Held throughout the year, college fairs allow students to talk to representatives from several colleges at once, as well as learn about colleges they haven't heard of before. Some college fairs include presentations on general topics, such as applying to college, testing, and financial aid. The *National College Fairs* of the National Association for College Admission Counseling give students a chance to talk to all kinds of colleges. NACAC offers a second, more specific set of *Visual and Performing Arts Fairs*.

If one of these free fairs isn't offered locally, counselors may want to offer one at their high school, since it can raise the visibility of college, and the counseling program, in the community. Putting one of these fairs together usually requires two steps:

1. Put in a request with the state college fair committee. Most states have a group that makes sure college fairs are scheduled in a way that doesn't burden the college reps who have to attend them all. The process of scheduling a college fair with them usually begins in the spring.

2. Organize a local arrangement committee. Counselors in neighboring schools often join together to send out the

invitations to colleges, reserve the facility for the event, secure student volunteers, arrange for refreshments, publicize, set up, and evaluate the fair. The location of the fair is rotated among participating schools.

Whether you send students to a NACAC fair or a local fair, it's important to prepare them to make the most of the experience. Share this advice, which is addressed to the student, and newsletter-ready:

With so many colleges at a fair, it's easy to get intimidated -- so plan ahead. Take a pen, a highlighter, an unofficial copy of your transcript, and five questions committed to memory that will help you learn more about a college. Ask about majors, food, chances for research, cost, social life-just make sure the answers will help you decide if this place is worth a closer look.

Once you're at a college booth, you might have to wait to ask questions—this is good! Use this time to listen to what the representative is saying to other students; since they will most likely be discussing general questions, you can use your time to ask for more detailed information.

Once it's your turn, get busy. "Hi, my name is (no student does this, but you should; it shows confidence and gives the rep the chance to remember you), and I go to Smith High School." From here, you want to ask your questions; make eye contact as they answer, and don't rush them.

If you like what you hear, pull out your transcript and say, "Just one more question. I'm putting my senior schedule together. Here's what I've taken so far; what other courses would your college like to see me take?" *Not many students do this*, which is why you should.

Thank them for their time, fill out a registration card (that's important), tell them you hope they come by your high school to visit, and move on. Make quick notes on this college *before* you visit the next booth—you don't want to confuse your colleges.

If you can do about seven to ten colleges and spend time at an information session of interest, you now have a good idea which colleges are worth visiting.

Notes and Follow-Up

- Look at the *National College Fairs* and *Visual and Performing Arts* fair schedules, and see what NACAC fairs are held in your area. Add these fairs to your school and personal schedule.

- If your high school doesn't offer a college fair, find the college fair schedule for your state, and see if one is held at a nearby school. If one isn't offered, consider putting together a local arrangements committee, and working with your Counseling Advisory Committee to start one. If one is offered, consider offering to cohost the fair at your high school on a rotating basis. Working with a neighboring college fair is better than duplicating your efforts, since two fairs that are close together usually both have a poor turnout. That sends the wrong message about the importance of college to your students, your parents—and the colleges.

- If you do offer a college fair, give it a ten-minute assessment. What works well? What could work better? How is it advertised? Who attends? Who should attend that isn't attending? How is it covered in the media? Is there support the Counseling Advisory Committee could offer?

Chapter 21
TESTING, PART III

College admissions testing for junior year has two parts. In the fall, many juniors will take either the PSAT or Aspire. The factors counselors use to decide which test to offer in the fall are the same factors discussed in chapters 16 and 17. It's likely students will want more test prep options for the PSAT, since a high score could qualify them for the National Merit Scholarship program.

Most juniors will then take the SAT or ACT for the first time in the winter or spring. Many counselors advocate students take each test once and take the one they're most comfortable with a second time, which leads to more questions.

When should students first take the SAT or ACT? Both tests are designed to measure what students know in the spring of their junior year, so most students will first take the test at that time. Some juniors will start as early as December, and use the results to prepare to take one test a second time in the spring. This strategy usually works as long as the student has completed Algebra II; if they're not finished with Algebra II, there's a good chance part of the math they learn in winter of junior year will be on the tests, so a December score might not be as high.

How often should a student take the test? Generally, not more than twice. As a rule, scores on the third or fourth attempt are higher only if the student devotes significant extra time to intense test preparation, and even then, there's no guarantee.

What if the student needs a specific score for a merit scholarship? If a twenty-eight on the ACT qualifies the student for a scholarship, and they have a twenty-seven, another try makes sense—even if it's a third or fourth try—and the counselor should explain that to the college.

Do the colleges care how often a student takes the test? Most colleges let the student decide which test scores they send with their application. If that's the case, a student taking the SAT three times only has to send in their best results. Some colleges ask for all test results, and while no college has an official limit, some college admissions officers do worry a little about students who take the ACT or SAT four or five times—or more.

What is test superscoring? A college that superscores takes the best English score and the best math score from the SAT (or the best subscores from the ACT) even if they're from different test administrations. This increases the student's test scores and the college's average test score. The best way to find out if a college does this is to ask.

Does any college look at the student's lowest test scores? Colleges that require all of your test results say they only use the best results. Still, it's best to ask.

Should high schools submit test scores with transcripts? Many high schools no longer do this, since students want more control over which test results the colleges see, and more colleges only accept scores sent directly from the testing companies.

Some colleges will take unofficial scores; ask, and send them only when the student specifically requests that be done.

What about registering for testing accommodations for special needs? Students must apply for accommodations well in advance of the test date. This requires ample documentation, and often requires evidence the student uses testing accommodations at school as well. The test's websites have the latest on these policies.

Notes and Follow-Up

- The *ACT Test Information Release** service offers students the opportunity to get a copy of their test questions, their answer sheet, the correct answers, and other information on their test. Some students find this a helpful tool for test preparation, so take a look at the description (and test date limits) of this service.

- Review *ACT Services for Students with Disabilities* and *SAT Students with Disabilities* to make sure you understand the steps students and the school need to take to request testing accommodations. Review how this is communicated with students, parents, and staff—especially the special education faculty.

- Review your school's test prep program for eleventh grade testing; it may be very different from what tenth graders are offered. Look at the test prep material for SAT on *Khan Academy*, and for ACT on *Number2.com*. How can you incorporate these materials into your test prep efforts?

Chapter 22
SUBJECT TESTS,
AND TEST OPTIONAL COLLEGES

SAT Subject Tests are the lesser-known tests offered by SAT. About 160 colleges use Subject Tests in their admissions process. Of those, only a couple dozen require them; most of the other schools want test results from either the ACT with Writing, or the SAT and two Subject Tests. A few others recommend students take Subject Tests; generally, that should be read as a requirement, if the student is serious about the college.

The good news about Subject Tests is that they offer students some flexibility. Subject Tests are an hour long, and given at the same test sites that offer the SAT Reasoning Test. This allows students to take up to three Subject Tests in one sitting—which works well, since most colleges requiring them want students to submit the results of two Subject Tests. In addition, many colleges allow students to choose which subjects to take out of the twenty Subject Tests that are offered. Many engineering programs will require students to submit scores for the Math II test and/or a science test, and other programs may require specific tests; it's always best to check.

Students usually take Subject Tests right after they complete the class they're taking in that area, since that is when they know the most about the subject. For most students, that means they take them at the end of junior year, but some students will take them at the end of ninth or tenth grade, if that's the last grade where they will take a subject such as biology, chemistry, or history. The six language tests that include a listening portion are only offered in November; the non-listening tests in many languages are only offered in June. Students will want to check the *College Board Subject Test* website for the schedule, and for sample questions of each subject.

Concern that the results of one or two tests play too much of a role in college admissions has led many colleges to review their admission policies to determine if the test results really provide additional information on a student's academic potential. These reviews have led many colleges to create a test-optional admissions policy, where most students can decide whether or not to submit test scores as part of the admissions process.

Some of these test-optional colleges may require the submission of test scores to place admitted students into freshmen classes, to award scholarships, to determine athletic eligibility, or to admit students into more selective programs. *Fair Test (Fair Test Optional)* has a list of test-optional four-year colleges. Students will want to confirm this information on a college's website.

Students considering applying test-optional to a college should remember that the other parts of their application receive greater attention when test scores aren't submitted. This usually puts much more importance on the grades the student has earned, and the strength of the student's schedule, since the transcript is now the only indicator of the student's academic performance.

Students going test-optional may also want to consider asking the teachers who are writing letters of recommendation to put a special focus on their performance in class. While all teacher letters should address this important topic, the teacher's description of what the student has learned, and how they have learned it, plays a greater role with a test-optional applicant.

Finally, students with strong test scores should remember they *can* submit their test scores to a test-optional college; they just don't have to.

Notes and Follow-Up

- Review the list of *Institutions Using Subject Tests*, and make note of the colleges in your state that use them, as well as the colleges many of your students apply to that use them. This is good information to review before conducting your junior reviews.

- Look at the *College Board Subject Test* website to review the sample test items offered for each Subject Test. Will this be enough test prep for your student taking Subject Tests?

- Read the *Fair Test Optional* list of colleges, and note the colleges in your state (as well as those popular with your students) that don't require test scores for admission. Write a one-hundred-word article explaining test-optional schools to your students, and place it in your newsletter folder.

Chapter 23
JUNIOR INTERVIEWS

The college counseling curriculum has two goals: to provide strong, personalized college information to each student and their family, and to give the counselor information about the student's interests, abilities and goals so the counselor can help the student make a good college choice. In many cases, counselors find it easy to create ways to get information out to students—but due to high caseloads and non-counseling duties, some counselors are challenged to find the time to get information back from them.

The junior interview is a key checkpoint in this two-way communication process. Usually completed in January or February, the interview is often scheduled to review a student's senior year schedule, or review the student's progress toward graduation. Both these activities are important, but not necessarily time consuming. With a little advance planning, the twenty minutes many counselors spend on a graduation audit can become a five-minute review, leaving fifteen minutes to focus on the student's plans for life after high school.

Fifteen minutes may not seem like much time to understand the details of a student's college plan, but it can provide a strong start:

Before the meeting, the counselor provides the student with a printout of their progress toward graduation. Reviewing these requirements only becomes part of the interview if the student's progress leaves some requirements unfulfilled by their senior schedule.

Before the meeting, the counselor sends students a questionnaire that asks them to write down their proposed senior schedule, and information about their college plans. The questionnaire should also ask students to write down the questions they have about college, and give students a chance to share any unusual circumstances in their school experience (illness, personal challenges, etc.) Many counselors will also include questions for parents to answer.

The student will need to return this completed questionnaire to the counseling office at least a couple of days before the meeting. This gives the counselor time to review the schedule and the college answers, and prepare for the meeting. This is also the start of the student's commitment to timeliness, a must in the college application process. If the form isn't submitted on time, the appointment is rescheduled.

At the meeting, the counselor and student spend five minutes reviewing the student's progress toward graduation and their senior schedule. Some eager students will start the meeting with questions about their college plans. When that happens, make the most of their enthusiasm, and save the last five minutes to talk about their schedule.

The college portion of the meeting should include a brief review of the questionnaire, where the student has talked about their plans for visiting colleges, taking required tests, and asking for letters of recommendation. The rest of the time should be a discussion in which the student talks about what they are looking for in a college. Since this information is likely to be incomplete (they only know their intended major, but not how big a college they want, or where it's located), use the time to expand on those ideas, using the student's answers on the questionnaire as a guide.

The end of the meeting addresses the student's questions, and reviews any information either the counselor or the student needs to follow up with after the meeting.

With the right approach, counselors can explore the student's history, answer their questions, and offer support for the next steps the student needs to take, in a remarkably short period of time.

Notes and Follow-Up

- You're about to talk to a junior about college for the very first time. The student has made a tenth grade campus visit and attended the tenth grade college night. Write down all the other information you'd like to know about this student in order to help them him or her build a first college list.
- Take that list of information, and determine:
  - which information you already have.
  - which information the student could provide on a questionnaire.
  - which information you would want to discuss with the student in person.

Chapter 24
WORKING WITH FAMILIES

College counseling is a little different from most other counseling. While a great deal of therapeutic-based counseling models behavior, and allows students to work alone on their development, friends, colleges, parents, and the community as a whole are often taking an active role in where a student goes to college.

While the student is the client, counselors have relationships with others that impact the work with the client. In most cases, the parents are clearly the most interested and the most active, second only to the student (we hope!). Working with families in the college selection process becomes challenging because of the different combinations of interactions. A tenth grade college awareness activity is just for the student; a paying-for-college night program usually finds only the parents in attendance. If the dream college that was a shoo-in has said no, the meeting that follows is almost definitely going to be attended by both.

So different students with different interests and different needs have different family dynamics that come to us in different combinations at different times of the year, when the student's college plans are likely to be different. In the midst of all this difference, what has to be the one constant?

Working with the family to create a goal for their college-bound student, and sticking to it.

A good way to begin the process is to make sure families attend college awareness events as families. This is where coordinating efforts with feeder middle schools is essential. Whatever activities the schools organize, high school counselors need to participate in them once in a while, so parents can get a sense of continuity: when students go on to high school, the counselor will know what college activities families have seen, done, and thought about in middle school, and that will give parents a great sense of relief.

Maintain this same family focus in awareness activities during ninth and tenth grade. It's wise to use health classes and other class time for group guidance in college selection, but cement it with a couple of activities the whole family can go to, on nights, on weekends, online, and away from school.

Because many parents are busy, they just can't get to school—so bring the program to them. The library, an empty storefront downtown, the bowling alley, a place of worship, the country club, someone's home—all will work. Think about where parents will be most comfortable receiving the message; for many parents who went to the high school their children now attend, that high school is *not* the place. Changing things up keeps their attention.

In junior year, it's time to help the family focus in on the needs of the individual student. Begin by asking for some general information from students and their parents. Have them complete separate surveys, on paper or online. If the student and the parents aren't in agreement about college, follow this up with meetings (either just parents, just student, or together), where everyone can at least agree on a general direction for the student's college plans, and where to go from here. Follow this up with a thank-you note or e-mail, outlining the goal everyone has agreed on, and the foundation has been laid.

Notes and Follow-Up

- Contact the counselors at your feeder middle schools, and explain your interest in creating a sense of continuity in the college counseling message students hear in middle and high school. Invite them to your ninth grade parent night; it's more than likely they'll invite you to their eighth grade program as well.

- Think back on three students you've worked with whose families were closely involved with the student's college choice. In your opinion, what did they have in common, and what was different about them? Was there anything that, as a group, made them different from most other students you worked with?

- Now run a quick data disaggregation on these same three families. What does the data tell you about these families that may be helpful in planning your work with future students whose families may need more individualized attention in the college-selection process?

Chapter 25
BIG GROUND RULES

Counselors won't have to spend many (or any) college counseling sessions with every individual family, but they do need to make sure every family—that's student and parents—knows some key information. These issues are the source of most conflicts between counselors and college clients, so put them in newsletters, post them on the counseling website, include them in the college handbook for every grade, and feature them in the Junior Night program in the spring. It's worth the effort.

What follows is already in newsletter format, so just give me credit if you choose to use it.

My client is the student. Yes, I also want to support and work with my students' parents, since they are a big part of the team. But they aren't going to college—the student is, and I have to help get them ready. Let's work together to make sure that happens.

Let the student drive. This metaphor comes from an admissions officer at a highly selective college, who was asked for the best piece of advice to give parents. The college selection process is an opportunity for students to practice the leadership and autonomy skills they need to be successful in college. Parents don't take their child's turns at bat, or perform the bassoon solo for them at the state competition. That's why the student calls the college with questions and writes their own essays, and parents don't pretend to be the student when e-mailing questions.

Use college rankings sparingly. Unless your student was personally interviewed by a major magazine, published college rankings aren't based on their particular interests, goals, and needs. The list we build together will do that, and it's best to start that list from scratch.

A starter list is six to eight colleges long. This will vary greatly from student to student, but most of the time, students make great college choices if they walk into the first day of senior year with the names of two colleges they'll get into for sure, two colleges where they won't need significant financial aid, two colleges in their home state (just in case), and two dream schools. These can overlap, but that's what works for many students.

Most colleges don't like resumes. Believe me, if a college wants a piece of information about you, it will ask for it; if you give them too much of what they don't want, that makes an impression you don't want to give. All of the information on a resume is already in most college applications; if you have something else you want to tell the colleges, ask me about it.

Waive your FERPA rights. The Family Educational Rights and Privacy Act says, among other things, that you can see the teacher letters and counselor letters that are part of your college applications *once they become part of your student record at the college you attend.* FERPA does not require the high school to show them to you; the same is generally true for colleges that don't admit you. That said, it's best to waive your right; these letters are written *about* you, not *to* you, and not waiving your right leads some colleges to wonder why you don't trust your letter writers.

Deadlines are real. Colleges want complete applications by the date on the form. The College Counseling Office needs one school week to send a transcript. Testing agencies need a month to send test scores, and letter writers need three weeks to write a good letter. I'm a great counselor, but I can't move back the clock. Learn to plan ahead.

Notes and Follow-Up

- This is a starter list that's common to most schools, but not all schools. What items would you add? What items would you take out? Which ones would you mention in your Junior Night program?

- One other issue is final transcripts. To make sure students don't make enrollment deposits at more than one school, some schools have a policy that they send only one final transcript. Since there are legal issues involved with this policy, check on this with your school attorney before you decide to start this policy, or even promote it.

- The same is true for revealing discipline records of students. If a college asks about suspensions and discipline, what does your school tell them? This is a legal question, so get a legal opinion.

- Outline all of the ways you can share this information with your high school families.

Chapter 26
BUILDING A COLLEGE LIST

Many students will come to their junior interview with a clear idea of where they want to apply to college. It may be a college they've researched carefully that offers everything they're looking for; it may be the school one of their parents attended; it may be a college that sent them an amazing text or a colorful flyer in the mail.

This is both good news and bad news. The good news is that the student has made some kind of connection with a college. It's usually easier to work with this student than a student who arrives for their junior interview having never set foot on a college campus, with no idea what college is all about, or what makes one different from the other. Having the name of a college makes the student more likely to think about what they're looking for in their next school, and that's where a strong conversation can begin.

The bad news is that the student's interest in the college may not be based on their interests or abilities. The e-mail with a picture of a stunning oak tree in full fall color may lead the student to conclude the college is a perfect fit, even if it doesn't offer the criminal justice degree the student wants to attain. More important, the college may offer everything the student wants, but the student's chances for admission are small, because of the student's academic record, or because the college is incredibly popular, and very few applicants are admitted, even if they are highly qualified.

There are many factors involved in a good college decision, but the most important is fit—the idea that a college has to feel right to a student, and offer them the right mix of opportunity, challenge, and support. When a student brings the name of a college to their junior interview, this is their first attempt at exploring fit.

This gives the counselor a chance to talk with the student about what they're looking for, using the college as an example. "Tell me what you see here that you like" is a great conversation starter, giving the student the opportunity to talk about every good quality of that college. The student's description may also include some qualities that are not perfect, which can include anything-- distance from home, cost, or quality of social life.

It's likely their answer will give a strong sense of what the college experience means to the student, as well as the qualities that mean the most to them. This is important, since most students need to apply to more than one college—especially if they aren't completely sure what they're looking for, or if they have competing interests.

A complete investigation of these qualities will guide the counselor in the task of expanding the student's list of colleges in the right way, creating a list of colleges with different opportunities, costs, locations, and levels of admissibility. This gives the student the opportunity to keep their college options open for as long as possible, and that is an important point to share with them.

Too many students are convinced they have to start the first day of senior year knowing the college they'll attend, or knowing everything they are looking for in a college. In building the list through the junior interview, counselors can give stressed students permission to expand the search, take their time, and look far and wide at all of the options. This is the counseling part of college counseling, and it's vital.

Notes and Follow-Up

- It's good to be familiar with some of the college search programs students use to build their first college list. In addition to the college searches on subscription sites, such as *Naviance* and *Career Cruising*, students use sites like *Big Future, Cappex, Chegg,* and *College Express.* Use one or two of these websites to conduct a college search, using the same criterion. How are the recommendations different on each site?

- Counselors also use college guides such as *Rugg's Recommendations*, *Fiske Guide to Colleges*, *College Express Lists and Rankings*, and *College Lists Wiki* to help develop college lists for students. Review each of these sources, and consider how you might use them in working with your students. Would you share these resources with your students? Why or why not?

Chapter 27
STARTING WITH A HIGH CHOICE

In terms of admissibility, colleges in the United States run from **open** (where all students who apply are admitted) to **moderately selective, selective**, and **highly selective** (where less than 20 percent of all applicants are admitted). Given the recent history of admissions at a few colleges, some counselors have created the **überselective** category (coming from the German word über, or extremely), where the college admits less than 10 percent of all applicants.

A remarkable number of juniors begin their search interested in a college where their admission is less than a sure thing. These students usually have no problem explaining why they like this college, but they often have difficulty understanding why there's no guarantee they will be admitted. Students with grades and test scores lower than the college's average often point out the other qualities they have to offer that will make them attractive to the college, especially if the school claims it practices a *holistic* review of an application, a process that includes a close look at extracurricular activities, achievements, essays, and letters of recommendation.

Whenever a student applies to a college where admission is in doubt, it's important to be honest with the student, while still being supportive. For students with credentials that are below the college's averages, a discussion of data can be a good start. "The average GPA of an admitted student was a 3.4, with an average SAT score of 1250. You have a GPA of 3.1, and an SAT of 1070. That doesn't mean you won't be admitted, but it's likely most applicants will be ahead of you in these important areas."

At this point, it's *very* important to offer some support to the student. "The college admitted students with grades and scores below the average last year, so this doesn't mean you shouldn't apply. We just want to make sure you have strong options to choose from when it comes time to make a college decision next spring." This can lead to a discussion of the qualities the student sees in the college that makes it attractive, and the counselor's suggestions for schools to add to the student's college list.

In expanding the student's list of college options, counselors want to make sure the student understands the counselor's interest in having the list grow. College choice can be a sensitive topic for many students, and too many students can leave their counselor's office soured on any college if they think the counselor has just told them they "can't get in." Sugarcoating the student's chances of admission isn't the right thing to do, but offering too little give-and-take in a genuine discussion of college options can make a student feel unsupported—something that can make it hard to work with the student and their family with any college application.

In the interest of maintaining a strong relationship with the student, it's important to spend more time engaging the student in a discussion of college options rather than providing them with a list of colleges where admission is more likely. Rushing the list suggests the counselor is "telling" the student where to apply, something the counselor should avoid at all costs, since it takes control of the college decision out of the student's hands.

Exploring the student's thoughts about a certain college, and about college in general, can lead to a clearer understanding of the admissions process, and the value of other options, including starting at another college and transferring to the student's first-choice school. Take the time to guide the student through the process. Lists of colleges can be e-mailed later; trust can't.

Notes and Follow-Up

- Go over the college guides and other resources you frequently use to help students build college lists. Which ones have data covering average GPA and test scores for colleges, and how recent is that information?

- **Cross-application schools** are colleges similar to another college a student is interested in. For example, Yale is a cross-application school for Harvard. *The Fiske Guide to Colleges** offers this information; see if your college guides do as well. If not, be sure to ask for this information from the college admissions representatives who come to visit your high school.

- *Unigo* offers student reviews of colleges. Pick three of the most popular colleges your students apply to, and read their Unigo reviews. Would you recommend this site to your families?

Chapter 28
HIGHLY SELECTIVE COLLEGES

Some students applying to highly selective and überselective colleges face a different challenge. Most students who apply to these colleges usually meet or exceed the very high standards for admission, and most are actively engaged in other activities that set them apart from their peers. A straight-A honors student with near-perfect ACT scores who started her own phone-app business at age twelve may find it hard to believe that students with these qualities are routinely denied admission. The student should be told they can certainly do the work, but the college simply runs out of room before it runs out of good students.

It's also true that students are regularly admitted to these colleges for reasons other than academics: their parents went there, and are significant donors, the student is a strong athlete, or the student is related to a famous person. These kinds of admissions decisions happen at other colleges as well; they are more notable at the highly selective colleges and beyond because these colleges get more attention from the media, and admit such a small percentage of students.

Advice for students looking at colleges that admit less than 20 percent of their applicants can go in any number of directions. First, it needs to be made clear to students early on that these schools generally look for students with something more than top grades. The number of "just plain good students" who make it to highly selective college campuses is small, compared to the number of students who offer something else, or something more. It's important to talk with students about this early in the college counseling curriculum—at least as early as ninth grade—so students can decide if they are willing to devote the extra hours to studying and activities that top achievement requires.

Second, students need to understand these colleges have distinct qualities. Too many students begin the college selection process by deciding they'll apply to the first ten or twelve colleges on a "Best of" list, without understanding the strengths of each school, and which ones best meet the needs and interests. Unless the publication interviewed the student, its criteria for "Best of" aren't likely to meet the student's criteria without close inspection, which would include a campus visit.

Third, students should avoid trying to "time" their application. Highly selective schools may need viola players now, but after every middle school parent reads the same online article about that need, viola players will be in excess supply in five years. Students are better off following their natural interests and talents in order to achieve high status in the state, country, or world, a quality that is often needed for admission to a highly selective school.

Finally, students will have to expand their list to include at least one college that admits more than 20 percent of its applicants. Students applying to a dozen or more highly selective schools can only do so much to gain admission to at least one college without adding a school that admits a larger percentage of applicants. Highly talented students should look into honors and residential programs at other colleges, since they usually offer a high degree of rigor and opportunities for independent research. Many of these programs also offer merit-based scholarships, leading some students to complete their undergraduate studies through one of them, and look at highly selective institutions for graduate school.

Despite the images conveyed in the media, there are more than four great colleges for everyone—and they aren't the same four colleges for anyone. All students need to know that.

Notes and Follow-Up

- Develop a list of the honors and residential programs available through colleges in your state. Make note of how (and if) the admissions requirements for these programs are different from admission to the college, and if the college awards merit money for high-achieving students. This information is good to have at hand when developing college lists with juniors.

Chapter 29
UNDERMATCHING

Counselors are used to working with students interested in colleges that may be asking for more academic potential than the student has demonstrated in high school. Only recently has the opposite problem come to the attention of the school counseling community—and most would argue fixing it is long overdue.

Undermatching occurs when a student applies only to colleges where they may not find a high level of challenge or opportunity that meets their potential to learn. Undermatching offers two challenges. First, students who undermatch risk attending a college where they may get a good education but may not have opportunities that could significantly advance their academic and professional careers. A standout student interested in political science may be missing out on internships, running a political campaign, or learning from leading scholars in the field by not applying to colleges that offer these opportunities. The theory they learn at the college they attend may be just as strong, but the overall learning experience is missing something, given these students' potential to learn more.

Second, recent studies suggest undermatching is more likely to occur with bright students who are either from low-income communities or the first in their family to go to college, or both. Many of these studies ask if this is because the student is deliberately undermatching to stay close to home and their support group, or if the counselors working with these students aren't encouraging them to apply to demanding colleges.

All counselors need to give undermatching careful consideration. On the one hand, low-income and first-generation students attending highly selective and überselective colleges often report feelings of isolation, loneliness, and lack of support in their college experience, increasing the likelihood they will either transfer or drop out of college all together. On the other hand, talented students from underserved backgrounds can make the most of a demanding college experience, provided they seek and receive the support they need, accept the challenge that comes with the attempt, and believe they can succeed.

An effective college counseling curriculum exposes all students to all college options, including an introduction to the benefits of colleges where admission rates are small. Counselors working with low-income and first-generation students will want to introduce this information early in their curriculum to students and parents—most likely in middle school—to maximize awareness.

In high school, counselors will want to make the most of the available data to be sure qualified students who may not see themselves as admissible to a highly selective college receive information on admission requirements, and especially on financial aid. Several highly selective and überselective colleges offer free or significantly reduced tuition and room and board to qualified low-income students. With affordability established, students may feel encouraged to pursue a college option they previously considered unattainable, especially if they understand they have the potential to succeed at a highly selective college, and know how to apply.

Counselors working with undermatching students will also want to research summer programs and special visitation programs many highly selective colleges offer low-income and first-generation students. By exposing these students to the atmosphere of a highly selective college campus, counselors will be in a better position to help them determine if the academic and social demands of a highly selective school are an opportunity they're ready for. This kind of support can only lead to a better college fit, no matter where the student ends up attending college.

Notes and Follow-Up

- The research on undermatching is in its early stages, but a good amount of the media coverage has appeared in the online media sources the *Chronicle of Higher Education* and *Inside Higher Ed*. Go to these websites and complete a site search with the key word of undermatching to find current reports. How does this information apply to students in your high school?

- Open your college admissions data from last year and review the college application and matriculation decisions of low-income and first-generation students. Do the same colleges keep coming up, regardless of academic ability?

- Review any follow-up study you complete with your alumni to add questions designed to determine if graduates felt they undermatched in their college choice.

Chapter 30
STUDENTS WITH LEARNING DIFFERENCES

All students benefit from the general advice counselors give about college readiness and college awareness, but some students (such as undermatchers and those interested in highly selective colleges) will need additional advice based on the mix of challenge, opportunity, and support they are looking for in a college—a mix that sets them apart from their fellow students. This is the part of the individualization of the college counseling curriculum in which every student gets an answer tailored to them, even while using the curricular tools available to all students. The next few chapters outline some approaches to take when working with students who have special college interests.

The number of colleges offering a wide array of services to students with learning differences has grown tremendously in the past ten years. Where special needs students once included only students who needed a little more time to finish the standard tests or essays given in class, it now encompasses everything from ADHD to students who need note takers to students with closed-head injuries, and more.

These changes mean that, just as counselors can't send the aspiring poet and the literary critic to the same college that has the label of "good English department," we also can't send the dysgraphic student and the ADHD student to a college just because "they work well with students with learning differences." It's always good to have somewhere to begin, and for many counselors, the college search for the special needs student begins with *K & W Guide to Colleges for Students with Learning Differences**. You want to use this book the same way you use *Rugg's Recommendations on the Colleges**—as a jumping-off point to put together a list of colleges for the student to explore. Special needs are so individualized, it's impossible for students to find a good fit without visiting. After you complete a search using all other typical factors (size, major, campus atmosphere, etc.), check *K&W* to see what it has to say about the school.

The next step is to have the student visit the campus. All of the usual rules of campus visits apply here, plus one more: the student and parents need to stop by the support services office (after calling ahead to make an appointment) to meet with someone who will, in this order, do the following:

1. Listen to what the student needs.
2. Describe how those needs could be met at that college.

It's important that this happens in that order. If the special services representative simply lists the services the college offers, the representative may be trying to fit the student into the school's existing services, rather than create services to match the needs of the student—and that's a significant difference.

Unlike other interviews, it's usually a good idea for the parents to be part of this process, after the student has had some time to meet with the special services staff. Parents generally tend to have a stronger sense of the student's history, and they are almost always more willing to talk about the student's needs than the student. Having said that, counselors should make sure to strongly encourage the students to advocate for themselves. Not only does this improve the degree of commitment the students will make to their own learning, it may—again, that's may—sway the admissions decision in their favor, since it's clear the students know who they are and what they need.

As is the case with all students, follow up with them after the visit, find out which colleges they did and didn't like, and then head back to the books to find cross-application schools for the ones the student liked.

Notes and Follow-Up

- Pick any three of the ten most popular colleges your students apply to, and review the description of special services students with learning differences on their website. How easy is it to access this information? Is it easy to compare services among the three schools?

- Meet with the special education faculty in your building, and ask them to share their perceptions of the college decisions made by the students they serve. What additional programs, services, or information could the counseling office provide to support these students in the college selection process?

- Review your alumni survey to determine if it's currently possible to disaggregate the responses of students with learning differences. If it isn't, consider adding a question that could make this possible (and do this with each special population we're discussing).

Chapter 31
MORE ON LEARNING DIFFERENCES

Three other points need to be mentioned when working with students with learning differences. First, if you find a school on the student's list that isn't mentioned in *K&W,* or may not get a good review for support, *don't* automatically take it off the student's list. A campus visit may show the college has just what the student needs or that the student is willing to work with what the college has to offer.

Second, the student needs to realize that not every class is going to have the same level of support, even at a college that has a great reputation for support. While colleges work hard to individualize curriculum, and there are services some colleges are required to offer by law, there's still a good chance one professor may offer the student every service, while another will offer none, and a couple will offer a few—and this is all in the same semester.

Make sure students know that the most user-friendly, special-support college will still have some flaws; they just need to be ready to handle those by learning to be strong self-advocates. Students with learning differences should use their campus visit to get a feel for how much self-advocacy they'll need to demonstrate. They'll need these skills no matter where they go, but some colleges require greater self-advocacy than others.

Third, before developing a list for this student, be very sure to discuss how much information the student (and family) wants to share with the college. Some counselors believe this is an ethical question; after all, if the student has only earned great grades with the help of special services in high school, doesn't the college deserve to know that?

The answer here isn't so easy. It could be that the student relied heavily on special services early on, but has needed them less in their later school years. It could be that the college schedule in which the student takes four or five classes that don't meet every day will allow them ample time to prepare without the use of special services (this is why a "one class at a time" college like Cornell College of Iowa or Colorado College is worth a good look for students with organizational challenges and study habits). It could be the student is looking at colleges with academic reputations where their natural abilities will serve them just fine—in other words, they might need lots of help if they're applying to a highly selective school, but if the environment and academic tempo is a little more relaxed at the school of their dreams, they might thrive.

Counselors should review the high school policies on disclosing information about learning differences to third parties. In a vast majority of cases, disclosure will depend on getting parental or student consent; in some cases, school policy may dictate what can and can't be shared, regardless of the family's wishes. This information should be clearly communicated to all families through your counseling website and your college handbook.

It's also vital to address this issue with individual students and their parents at least by the middle of junior year. This gives the counselor and the family time to call some colleges and get a sense of what each one has to offer for that student's particular needs. It also gives the counselor time to see how each college reviews students who discuss learning differences as part of the admissions process.

Notes and Follow-Up

- It isn't uncommon for parents of students with learning differences to search the web for resources to support their children. Do a web search with the phrase *colleges for students with learning differences* and select four links to review. Which of these support the programming and philosophy of your college counseling curriculum, and how will you share them with parents and students?

Chapter 32
ATHLETES

Athletes may be the one special population that must receive specific admissions information in the predisposition phase of the college counseling curriculum. For better or worse, many colleges begin unofficial, off-the-record recruiting in the early years of high school (or sooner). This means students interested in intercollegiate athletics need to be aware of the process sooner rather than later.

A great way to share this information is through evening presentations. Many schools invite student-athlete alumni who went through the experience to talk one year, and then invite a college coach to speak the next year. Students are often surprised to discover that most athletes in Division I athletics programs view their participation as a full-time job, and not just part of a larger college experience Division II or III athletes may enjoy. Hearing directly from those involved in athletics is the best way to bring that message home.

It's also important for students to understand recruiting. Students sometimes walk away from one conversation with a college coach, convinced they have a firm offer of a full-ride admission to the college and a place on the team for four years. Students need to know early that no verbal commitment has the force of writing (and even then, some written offers can be rescinded).

Most offers are made for one year only, and not all offers come with scholarship money. Along with the rules about when coaches can contact students, and when colleges can pay for the student to visit campus, students will want to familiarize themselves early with the *NCAA Guide for the College-Bound Student-Athlete*—and since the rules change often, they should check for updates every year.

In addition, students will want to stay on top of the eligibility requirements they have to complete in high school. Students looking at NCAA Division I or II programs must complete courses in specific academic areas and register with the Eligibility Center. These students must also earn a minimum score on the ACT or SAT.

Each high school creates its class Eligibility List and submits the list to the NCAA, and it has to be updated when new classes are scheduled or old classes are no longer offered. Each high school has an NCAA contact person, and often that person is a counselor. Make sure you ask all students in their junior interview if they plan to play sports in college (it isn't unusual to have a great swimmer or tennis player who isn't on the school team). Direct them immediately to the NCAA website, and send in their transcript to the Eligibility Center when the student requests it.

High school coaches have college contacts and information on elite summer sports programs that can affect a student's chances to play college sports. This is why it's important to have the athletic director on the Counseling Advisory Committee. Sports are often the one part of high school a student loves more than all others, and the best way to help the student keep that interest alive in college, even if it's in intramural play, is to keep in touch with the people who shape them into good athletes. For similar reasons, this is why the band director, art teacher, and special education director are also on the CAC.

Most recruited athletes are keenly aware of what they need to do to keep their college athletic dreams alive. Supporting those dreams, and the athletic dreams of all students, requires good counselor diligence.

Notes and Follow-Up

- By the middle of junior year, many college athlete hopefuls have developed a well-honed college list, but some are still looking for colleges. One way to provide that list is to use the *Big Future* college search, and select the Sports and Activities option. Select a gender and sport to develop a list and then change the division option under Show Levels. Spend ten minutes exploring this option.

- Spend ten minutes looking at the *NCAA Guide for the College-Bound Student-Athlete*, and put together a one-hundred-word article for your ninth grade newsletter explaining the site.

- Take ten minutes to check out the *NCAA Eligibility Center*, looking at the options for students and the options for high school administrators. If you don't know who your contact person is, find out, and consider inviting them to join the Counseling Advisory Council.

- It's important to note that many colleges are members of athletic organizations other than the NCAA. Check the college's website; if it is, review that organization's rules regarding eligibility and recruitment.

Chapter 33
ARTISTS

Like athletes, some artists will be admitted to highly selective programs because of their tremendous talents, even if their grades and test scores don't meet the college's averages. Like schools known for their programs for students with learning differences, a college that has a reputation for a strong art program may not have a very good ceramics program, or the ceramics teacher at that college may have an approach to teaching that doesn't fit with the student's creative bent.

This is why counseling artists requires the use of many counseling skills applied with other special populations. While artists don't have to pass NCAA muster, it's important to remember some colleges will admit students directly into art and music schools, but many others require artists to meet the admissions requirements of the university before they get a chance to audition or submit a portfolio. The amount of weight the portfolio or audition will play in admissions varies widely from college to college; it's important to find this out early in the list-building process, since some programs require no portfolio or audition at all.

Like the athlete, the artist also needs to have some sense of their commitment to the craft. Many artists spend the entire first semester of college in the studio, only to decide perhaps an academic major is worth consideration. That is easier to do at a university than it is at an art school, so building a list is simpler if a student has a clear sense of just how deep the art calling is for them.

For all these reasons, the campus visit is extremely important for the artist. In addition to taking the campus tour, students should make sure to call ahead for appointments to meet with representatives of the arts program. It may very well be these appointments are tied only to days when auditions and portfolio reviews are occurring, so they should be sure to call.

In addition, students will want to look at the depth of the college's program. Do they allow flute majors to study saxophone as well, or can engineering majors use the ceramics lab? They also want to ask about teacher training; many small colleges do not have the classes needed for arts students (or anyone else, for that matter) to become teachers. Since this can be a particular need for artists, it is always good to ask in the junior interview what plans the student may have about teaching to support their creative endeavors.

Two more points are important for artists. First, studio artists will want to take advantage of *National Portfolio Day*, an event where art schools travel as a group to offer advice on portfolios in progress. NPD is well attended, so some students get frustrated because they can only talk to one or two colleges; however, the feedback students can get on their portfolios is invaluable—and it's given by those who will review portfolios in the admissions process. This is a great program for seniors, an even better one for juniors.

Second, artists of all kinds will want to make note of the *NACAC Performing and Visual Arts College Fairs*. Here, arts program representatives from arts-focused colleges and general colleges and universities talk with students about what their schools have to offer in the arts.

In an age when college costs dictate what too many students choose as their major, it's still important to talk with artists about their plans for paying off college debt, and making a living. The student's answers may change over time, but starting the conversation is an essential part of good college counseling.

Notes and Follow-Up

- Pick two colleges in your state that offer music as a major. Review these admission requirements:
  - In addition to the general admissions requirements to the college, are there specific requirements for admission into the music program?
  - Is an audition required? If so, what are the requirements (not all auditions are the same!)?
  - Does the college offer music education as a major? If so, can the student major in both performance and education at the same time?
  - Can students transfer into the program as sophomores?
  - Are all music classes open to nonmusic majors?
- Pick two colleges in your state that offer art as a major, and review these admission requirements:
  - In addition to the general admission requirements to the college, are there specific requirements for admission into the art program?

- ○ Is a portfolio required? If so, what are the requirements (not all portfolios are the same!)?
- ○ Does the college offer art education as a major? If so, can the student major in both performance and education at the same time?
- ○ Can students transfer into the program as sophomores?
- ○ Are all art classes open to nonart majors?

- Review the *National Portfolio Day* schedule, and see if an NPD program is coming to your area. How will you share this information with your students?

- Talk with the fine arts faculty at your school. What trends, insights, and information do they give to students considering art as a major? Is help available at the high school for students developing a portfolio or audition piece?

Chapter 34
UNDOCUMENTED STUDENTS

The process of applying to college isn't always a walk in the park for many students, but the common complaints about finding time to write all those essays and needing to find more money for college pale in comparison to the challenges of the undocumented student. Consider these situations:

- A student is about to take the ACT or SAT, so they have to show a photo ID. No problem— the student pulls out their driver's license. Undocumented students?

- A student is applying to a college that asks if they are a US citizen. The student should check yes or no, whatever applies. What does an undocumented student check if they were born in the United States?

- It's time to apply for financial aid, so the student digs out their Social Security card and writes the number on the FAFSA. Undocumented students?

There is nothing automatic about these steps for undocumented students; each question requires research, and that takes extra time. It is especially challenging if the student hasn't told their high school counselor that the student is undocumented. By law, counselors cannot ask this question, and if they do not know, they are unable to provide the special assistance many undocumented students need in the college application process.

Most high school students are reluctant to ask questions or ask for help, and the experiences of many undocumented students often reinforce this tendency. This makes it all the more important for school counselors to provide college information to undocumented students and their families in ways they can access it without feeling they are risking their personal safety—and that usually means having access to it without asking for it. Successful approaches include the following:

Providing information as part of the general college counseling curriculum. It may go without saying, but it's highly unlikely anyone would attend an evening program titled "College for Undocumented Students." Information specific to undocumented students should be built into existing programs: make sure college admissions officers talk about the application process and scholarship opportunities for undocumented students at the school's college night, include an undocumented student on your alumni speaker's panel who is willing to share their story of going to college, and incorporate written information on the unique needs of undocumented students in the newsletters and websites all parents and students receive and view. Like all families, undocumented students and their parents need help with the college process; unlike many families, they can't call attention to their specific needs. This approach allows them to do that.

Promote the idea that college is possible for undocumented students. One exception to the "keep it in the curriculum" rule is promoting the idea that undocumented students can go to college. Posters displayed at school and videos posted on the counseling website are two of the many ways to make sure undocumented students and their families know college is in their reach. This information may need to be in more than one language, and the "think about college" message definitely needs to start well before high school.

Know the terrain of the colleges you recommend to undocumented students. Document status is only one of many factors undocumented students may want to consider in their college search, so it's important not to limit your help to colleges seen as friendly to undocumented students. At the same time, knowing if a college offers in-state tuition to undocumented students, asking the admissions representatives that visit your school about the services they offer undocumented students, and keeping abreast of any changes in state or federal law will make you a valuable resource when a student expresses interest in these options.

Notes and Follow-Up

- Many colleges provide ample resources offering advice for undocumented students that is both specific to their college and applicable to the college selection process in general. One such resource is the *Michigan State Undocumented Student Guide to College.*

- Two other resources rich with advice are the *IACAC College Advising Guide for Undocumented Students,* produced by the Illinois Association for College Admission Counseling, and *Firstgenerationstudent.*

- The above websites contain the answers to the three questions asked at the beginning of this chapter. Review these resources to find the answers, and consider how to spread the word to your students about these resources in a way that will protect their anonymity.

Chapter 35
LGBTQ STUDENTS

Due in part to significant cultural and legal changes, there is a wider array of self-acceptance and social acceptance than ever before of lesbian, gay, bisexual, transgender, and questioning youth. LGBTQ students raised in open homes in accepting communities may feel a degree of comfort and acceptance that was unimaginable a few short years ago, while the surroundings of other LGBTQ students require them to be (or lead them to believe they should be) less forward in discussing their sexual or gender identity and their related needs.

This wider range of acceptance reminds school counselors—and colleges—that the programs and services institutions offered to LGBTQ youth just a few years ago are no longer enough to meet the needs of an increasing special population. Effective college counseling requires counselors who keep up with the times; that can be done, and LGBTQ students can best be served, by doing the following:

Focus on the student as an individual. Since the talents, abilities, goals, and college interests of LGBTQ students are just as wide as those of all youth, the qualities they are looking for in a college go well beyond their sexual or gender identity. As is the case when working with any student, counselors need to focus on the whole student, and work with them to find a college that will offer the right mix of opportunity, challenge, and support for all aspects of their life.

"LGBTQ friendly" may not be an issue... Students should have an opportunity to share the importance of an LGBTQ-friendly campus without sharing their sexual or gender identity. This can be done as part of the questionnaire all students complete before the junior interview. By listing "LGBTQ-friendly campus" as one of many qualities a student can check in response to the question "What features are you looking for in a college?" the student provides the information the counselor needs, without having to talk to the counselor about what the student may see as a private issue.

...but transition may be. An LGBTQ student may not be interested in finding a college that is known for its support of LGBTQ students, but the student certainly wants to feel safe and respected on their college campus. Students identifying as LGBTQ to the counselor should be encouraged to investigate the campus climate they will be living with during their college years. This is especially true if the student is coming from a high school that is welcoming to LGBTQ students; the student may be so used to being completely accepted, they don't consider that the environment could be different at a college.

Campus tours are important for all students to complete as part of the college selection process, but this is particularly true for LGBTQ students. A firsthand look at the resources and programs offered LGBTQ youth, combined with the students' sense of the campus atmosphere, can make for a smoother transition to their new school.

Have resources at the ready. Students interested in exploring the services and programs a college offers LGBTQ students should be met with updated resources and information. Several websites offer reviews of these services by college, and college admissions officers should be able to provide detailed information on the programs and campus climate to students and counselors. Many of these resources should be made available through general newsletters and on the counseling website, increasing access to include students who wish to receive this information without discussing it with the counselor.

Notes and Follow-Up

- *Campus Pride* offers a wide array of articles and resources for LGBTQ youth, including the Campus Pride Index that assesses the LGBTQ friendliness of hundreds of colleges. Take a look at the reviews of the colleges in your state; having a sense of this information can be helpful in preparing for junior interviews and beyond.

- If Campus Pride doesn't review the most popular colleges your students apply to, review the websites of those colleges to see what services they offer LGBTQ youth.

- Review the membership of your Counseling Advisory Committee to make sure your counseling program is well connected to the programs and supporters of LGBTQ youth in your community.

Chapter 36
INTERNATIONAL STUDENTS

As is the case with every special population, there are no hard and fast rules that apply to every single international student. That said, there are at least a few logistical issues that seem to apply to a vast majority of students from other countries who wish to study in the United States:

More paperwork. Because international students have to complete an I-20 to attend any school in the United States, it's very likely they (or their parents) know exactly what to do to make sure the form follows them from high school to college. Counselors should know the person who oversees the I-20 paperwork for the high schools—and in a public school this may be someone at the district office.

More testing. Many colleges require non-English-speaking international students to take the TOEFL (or other test of English proficiency) as part of the admissions requirement. The *Test of English as a Foreign Language* * is generally required in addition to any other testing (SAT, ACT, etc.), but some colleges will waive the TOEFL requirement if the student has spent all of their high school years attending a US high school. Some colleges will also have a minimum TOEFL score the student must earn to be considered for admission.

More support programs. There has been an increase in the number of international students attending US colleges, leading to many colleges expanding the services and programs offered for this special population. Some colleges even offer specific programs for international students from one country or region, and these can include social as well as academic programs. This makes campus visits all the more important for international students. In some cases, students staying with host families or attending boarding schools may need assistance finding transportation to get to campus visits.

Fewer admitted. The increase in the number of international students applying to US colleges means there are more international students attending US colleges, but it also means more international students are being denied admission to US colleges. These increases mean the acceptance rates at some colleges may be lower for international students than for US students, just like the acceptance rates at many public universities are lower for out-of-state students than in-state students. Keep this in mind when creating college lists for international students.

Less financial aid. International students do not qualify for federal financial aid or for most state-based aid, leaving very few colleges that offer some financial support. It has been said one of the reasons international students were popular applicants during the Great Recession is that a vast majority of them had to pay the full cost of attendance, which helped the budgets of many colleges. Since then, more colleges are offering privately sourced aid to international students each year.

Same individual family dynamics. As discussed in chapter 24, all families come to the college selection process with questions, assumptions, and expectations, and the families of international students are no exception. Just like the college expectations of some—but not all—US families may be shaped in part by where the family lives, the college expectations of some—but not all—international families may be shaped in part by where the family lives. Counselors will best serve international students by listening closely to the needs and interests of the family on an individual basis, just as the best interests of US students are met, and by offering appropriate support.

Notes and Follow-Up

- Do a data review to determine the three most popular college choices of your international students. Review the international student information on the websites of those three colleges, and call the admissions officers to ask for their advice on how to counsel international students applying to their college. Are the admission rates at these schools for international students different from the rates for US students?

- Take a look at the *TOEFL* website to get an understanding of how this test is different from the SAT and ACT, especially in terms of administration options.

- If the college websites didn't say so, look at the financial aid web pages of these colleges to see what resources each school offers international students.

- *Schools Awarding Financial Aid InternationalStudent. com* will take you to an updated list of colleges known to give financial aid to international students. Review the list, and note the colleges that are popular with your international students.

116

- The international students who attend your school may know English, but their parents may not. Is there a need for the college counseling office to offer some materials in a language other than English?

Chapter 37
COMMUNITY COLLEGE

Two special college choices may come up for the first time in the junior meeting.

First, if anything good came out of the Great Recession, it was a newfound respect for the value of community colleges. Long seen as the stepchild of higher education, economic necessity led a number of families to understand that community college is "real college." Because some of these stereotypes still exist, it's important for counselors to help students building a college list consider how community college can advance their academic goals.

Community colleges typically serve three purposes. The **vocational** purpose of community college is to help students secure the training, certification, and licensure they need to enter certain careers. Students attending community college for this purpose will take few, if any, general education courses. Their curriculum will be focused on courses that give them job-related skills or knowledge needed to pass related professional exams. Students who want to attend trade school or for-profit schools offering career training may have been told at some point they shouldn't consider college. If that's the case, the counselor will want to encourage them to look into community colleges as an alternative to trade school. A community college could be closer to home, and is more affordable.

The **preparatory** purpose of a community college is to give students an opportunity to improve their academic skills before taking classes that will lead to an associate's degree or a transfer to a four-year institution. Long seen as part of the adult education division of local public schools, these literacy classes have become a larger part of community college's offerings, due to budget cuts in K-12 education. These offerings have led to the perception that community college "isn't real college," but the courses have helped thousands of students achieve new levels of academic and economic success and self-esteem.

The **transfer purpose** of a community college allows students to begin their work toward a bachelor's degree. Working closely with both a community college counselor and a transfer counselor at the student's destination college, the student selects courses that will not only transfer to their next college, but will also meet specific requirements for the degree the student is seeking at that institution. *Articulation agreements and 2+2 plans* often streamline this process, outlining all of the courses that students can complete at a community college to meet requirements at their next institution.

Students who want to start their postsecondary education careers at a community college should work closely with a community college counselor to make sure their course selections are advancing their academic goals; sharing this at the senior meeting is a must. Too many students simply enroll in classes at the local community college, assuming the classes will transfer to their next college. They may transfer, but if the next college simply accepts them as elective credit, the student will find they have to spend more time and money taking additional classes that meet degree requirements. Other students assume courses they've completed on a community college's preparatory track will transfer to four-year colleges—an assumption that is almost always untrue.

High school counselors will want to work closely with community college-bound students to make sure they understand the importance of seeing a community college counselor or adviser on a regular basis. High school counselors will want to offer the same advice to all students who may be participating in an early college program or to students planning on taking community college classes in the summer, after starting at a four-year institution. Many four-year colleges limit the credits these students can transfer from a community college, even if the classes meet degree requirements. Students will want to make the most of their time and money; high school counselors can help them do both.

Notes and Follow-Up

- Students and parents are only going to see community colleges as a viable college choice if they are mentioned in your programs and newsletters. Select a few newsletters at random; how many times are community colleges mentioned when talking about college?

- Review the list of colleges that come to visit your high school. How many are community colleges? Contact the admissions offices of the community colleges that should visit your high school.

- Review the list of college admissions officers who present at your high school's college nights and other college programs. How well are community colleges represented? How can you better include them in existing programming or in new programming?

- Review the websites of five of your most popular four-year colleges to see if they offer merit-based transfer scholarships for community college students or community college graduates.

- *Phi Theta Kappa Scholarships* are available through the nation's most recognized community college honors society. Review the list for scholarships available through colleges your students attend.

Chapter 38
GAP YEARS

A growing number of US students are interested in taking some time off before they start college. Having worked hard in high school to be admitted to a college that's right for them, some students may want some time to recharge, rejuvenate, or learn about the world outside the classroom before returning to the classroom.

One option these students can pursue is to take a **gap year**, or planned time off between high school and college. Unlike students who get to the end of senior year and start to wonder if college is really the right choice, gap year students generally find a program, opportunity, or life experience they'd like to pursue that might not be available to them once they start college. This can include teaching English in another country, working with a nonprofit social agency, organized travel, career exploration organized by a gap year agency, or working to earn more money for college.

The process for taking a gap year is relatively simple. Students apply to colleges in their senior year as if they were planning to attend the following fall—they do not, and should not, mention they plan on taking a gap year. Once they're admitted, they contact the college and explain their interest in deferring admission for a year or six months. Colleges that allow students to take a gap year typically ask for an enrollment deposit and give the student a deadline to notify the college if they aren't coming—and that's it.

Some school counselors will promote the idea of a gap year as part of their college counseling curriculum. At the same time, most students who feel the need for a gap year usually find their way to a program or experience they're interested in, taking the initiative to make sure their colleges of choice will let them defer.

Given that track record, some counselors hesitate to present the idea of a gap year to a wider audience, since some students may misunderstand it as "a year off," which puts them in danger of never going to college or delaying the development of career skills. Students who discuss a gap year with their counselor in the spring of junior year (or fall of senior year) have put in the thought and energy needed to investigate gap year options and create the opportunity. Students with firm college plans who come to your office two days before graduation to talk about a gap year may just be coming late to the party. More likely, they are having second thoughts about their college choice, or about leaving high school. It's important to give each case the counsel it deserves.

Colleges granting deferred admission often require the student not to use the year to attend another college, and many will also freeze the student's financial aid package—something to consider if a tuition increase will require the student to find more money for school. While more private colleges allow students to take a gap year, some public colleges will as well.

A handful of gap year students may inform you they plan on applying to college after they complete their gap year. This is generally a bad idea; not only is the student out of high school, making contact with counselor and teacher recommenders more challenging, but the student could also be out of the country, making contact with the college more challenging. A gap year is an opportunity to learn in a new way, not cut corners in applying to college. If that's the student's goal, it's time to have a different conversation.

Notes and Follow-Up

- Consider where you would introduce the idea of a gap year to your students and families. Write a one-hundred-word article on gap years, and drop it in your newsletter file.

- *USA Gap Year Fairs* runs a nationwide series of fairs featuring a wide array of gap year options. Take a look at the schedule; if a fair is being offered near you, add it to your school and counseling calendars.

- The Gap Year Programs heading under *USA Gap Year Fairs* offers information on a number of gap year programs. Investigate three of these programs, and consider the benefits they could offer your students.

Chapter 39
THE TWENTY-MINUTE MEETING

Just about the time junior meetings begin, counselors want to get parents and students talking to each other about college on a regular basis. This isn't something they are likely to start doing on their own. Many teenagers are looking for autonomy from their parents when it comes to big decisions, and parents brave enough to reach out to their student can usually benefit from some encouragement and advice on what to talk about, when to talk about it, and how to persist if the student offers resistance.

Enter the twenty-minute family meeting. By suggesting that juniors meet weekly with their parents to discuss college plans for twenty minutes, the counselor is stressing the importance of communication among family members. This emboldens parents who want to get a handle on their child's thoughts about college, and it softens the student's aversion to talking with their parents about a choice as personal as college. Once introduced to the idea, most students will take on the task, saying "OK, as long as this is the only time we talk about college all week."

That is exactly the purpose of the twenty minute meeting. Despite their best hopes, students actually know they have to talk to their parents about college anyway. When it's time to pay for a college test, they need money; when they want to attend a

125

college open house with friends, they'll need to tell them; when students are staying in their rooms for prolonged periods of time to write essays, telling their parents nothing is wrong is the right thing to do. Meeting once a week at the same scheduled time (usually on weekends, with parents providing snacks) is at least a guarantee that Mom and Dad won't embarrass them by asking the wrong college question at the wrong time, since the only time they get to ask questions is during the meeting.

That is the single biggest challenge for Mom and Dad: they only get twenty minutes each week to address their college questions. A big part of the buy-in from students comes from knowing they are being responsible to their parents by talking about college, while also getting their independence for the rest of the week. There are likely to be times when the "meeting only" rule has to be broken (often when applications are due), but parents need to demonstrate trust in their child, who is taking a big step toward starting their own life.

Another challenge is making sure parents and students have something to talk about at each twenty-minute meeting. Counselors can offer support, and a sense of flow to the weekly meetings, by suggesting topics to discuss at the end of each junior and senior newsletter. With a little forethought, counselors can create a sequence of questions that mirrors the work they are doing with the juniors at school. This creates a sense of mutual reinforcement that makes student, parents, and counselor a team with a common purpose clear to all.

Parents in some communities may feel the need to start the twenty-minute meeting early in the junior year; for most schools, starting in the middle of the junior year is a good place to begin.

The meeting takes a recess in the summer and then starts again in the fall of senior year, usually lasting until the student puts a deposit at the college of their choice.

Notes and Follow-Up

- Brainstorm college topics you would want parents and students to discuss as a family in the junior and senior years.
  - What are they?
  - What sequence should the topics follow?
  - What information would you give parents and students to introduce each topic to them before they discuss it with each other?
- This list now serves as the basis for most of your junior and senior newsletters.

Chapter 40
STUDENTS AND TEACHER LETTERS OF RECOMMENDATION

Junior meetings should also address letters of recommendation. As a rule, colleges that ask for teacher letters like to see two, written by teachers who have worked with the student in eleventh or twelfth grade. With so many college application deadlines being moved up to the fall of senior year, it's usually best to choose teachers from junior year, since senior year teachers may have only worked with the student for a few weeks when the letter is due. Some students will ask senior year teachers they have also worked with in ninth or tenth grade, and that can be a real bonus, since the teacher can speak to the student's growth over time.

In terms of whom to ask, colleges usually require letters from teachers of academic subjects. Some programs (especially engineering) will want to hear from at least one math or science teacher, but most will leave this up to the student. Many counselors suggest students ask one math or science teacher for a letter, and ask for another letter from a teacher of English, social studies, or language. Many colleges used to have this requirement, and some counselors maintain it's the best way to see how students work in very different academic areas. Other counselors will simply encourage the student to ask the two academic teachers who best know the student, as long as the teachers haven't worked with the student in the same subject—and science is usually considered one subject.

As students consider who to ask, it will be important to make sure they understand that the purpose of teacher letters is to show colleges what it's like to work with them in a classroom on a regular basis. Does the student have good work habits? Are they curious about the subject, and if so, how do they show it? Do they work well with others? Do they participate in class discussion? Have they engaged in independent research?

By answering these questions, the teacher is bringing the reader of the recommendation letter into their classroom and letting the reader see the student in action—and that's the goal. It's wonderful if the teacher has also worked with the student as a coach, adviser, or club sponsor, but those are extra dimensions. Focusing on those encounters at the expense of showing the academic side of the student makes for a weaker letter.

Students also need to remember that writing a good letter of recommendation takes time. Many counselors encourage juniors to ask for letters of recommendation in mid-May of junior year. This gives the teachers the opportunity to write the letters over the summer, or at least organize their writing time in the fall once school starts. If a student has to ask in the fall, they need to understand why a teacher might get upset if the student asks for a letter on Tuesday that the colleges want that Thursday. Three weeks' notice is a minimum for last-minute letters.

As students consider which teachers to ask, they'll often say the adult who knows them best doesn't teach an academic subject, or teach at all. Most colleges will accept an extra letter from a coach, religious leader, boss, or other teacher, as long as the letter will add another dimension to the story the application is telling. If a college won't accept more than the required number of letters, the student can ask the adult who knows them best to give some comments to the counselor to add to the secondary school report.

Notes and Follow-Up

- Review the letter of recommendation requirements of the five most popular colleges your students apply to. Are they the same for all programs of the college?

- Look up the letter requirements for three additional colleges that offer engineering as a major. Do they ask for letters from specific teachers?

- Do the same for three music schools, and three art schools. Do they require a letter from the instructor in the student's intended major?

- Look at your school calendar and consider what time in the spring would be best for juniors to start asking for letters of recommendation. Ask the teacher members of your Counseling Advisory Committee for their thoughts on this issue.

Chapter 41
TEACHERS AND TEACHER LETTERS OF RECOMMENDATION

The single biggest challenge with letters of recommendation is limiting their number. Students, parents, and teachers often think more letters are always better, but that just isn't the case. Relaying detailed information is certainly important, but doing so in eight letters of recommendation, when the college asks for two, can be counterproductive. The college will read all of them, but may discount the value of the extra letters, especially if they are written by someone who does not know the student well, or if they emphasize what another letter has already said. This may not hurt the student's chances of admission, but it certainly won't help them.

Another challenge when working with teachers is guiding them on the content of the letter they write. It's easy to understand why teachers may take exception to a counselor trying to tell them how to write a good letter of recommendation. At the same time, our job is to make sure all parts of the application put the student in the best possible light.

With that as our goal, it's important for teachers to get an annual reminder about these do's and don'ts, presented here in newsletter-ready style:

Don't list the student's extracurricular achievements. Colleges want you to tell them what you know about working directly with the student in the classroom. If you've happened to work with them as a coach or adviser, you can talk about that relationship, but keep the focus on the classroom. Since the student has told the college about their awards and activities, keep that list out of your letter completely. You only have a page; make the most of it.

Don't talk too much about your teaching background It certainly helps colleges put your comments in context if they know you've been teaching for three years or thirty years. That's something you can add at the very end of your letter; start the letter with the strongest words of support and praise you can offer about the student.

Do tell stories about the student. Nothing brings a letter of recommendation to life for a college like a description of the day the student turned in that incredible paper, or offered a powerful insight in class discussion. Adjectives only convey so much about a person; telling a story about an event brings the college right into your classroom.

Don't agree to write a letter if you can't write a good one. Students are asking you to write a letter of recommendation because they believe your letter will offer strong reasons for the college to admit them. If you don't think you can honestly write that letter, it's better to tell the student that, and give them the chance to find another teacher who can.

Don't turn your letter in late. Just as you need every student's paper by a certain deadline, colleges need every student's letters by their deadline. Colleges know teachers are busy, but being late with a letter should be a rare occurrence. If you can't meet the deadline, gently direct the student to another teacher.

Many counselors send this information as an e-mail at the start of the year, while other counselors invite a college admissions officer to give a presentation to the faculty on letter writing. They are usually happy to do so, and there is nothing like faculty hearing the do's and don'ts directly from the person who will read the letters they write.

And yes, the letter is a page. As one college representative said, if there's something so important it needs to go on page two, it really should be on page one.

Notes and Follow-Up

- Review your school's policy on whether or not students can see letters of recommendation before they are submitted. Most high schools don't allow this, and don't have to—but do students, parents, and teachers know that? If so, how are they told?
- Review the way the counseling office keeps track of which teachers are writing for which students. Is this information easy to access by the student? By the teacher?

Chapter 42
SENIOR YEAR

The college counseling curriculum of twelfth grade quickly turns into a massive swirl of individualization. College lists will change, deadlines will pop up on the most organized of students, and parents will need to be told, again and again and again, that everything will be OK. In the midst of all of this, students will rush in with news of college acceptances and scholarship offers that weren't even on their final list. Dickens didn't realize it, but he was describing the fall of senior year in a college counseling office when he wrote "It was the best of times, it was the worst of times." It's impossible to stay organized, but it's wonderful to experience.

There are about three weeks at the start of the school year to organize before chaos descends. By making the most of that time, the college counseling needs of half of your class will be met, no matter how large your caseload.

To begin with, don't forget the newsletters. The senior newsletters keep students and parents on task and on time, and at this point, that's all the most organized seniors—about 10 percent of the class—will need. Pick the same day of the week to publish the newsletter, and don't go home until it's done.

It's also important to find a way to touch base individually with each senior to double-check graduation requirements, ask about college plans, talk about sending test scores (the student's job), and check on letters of recommendation (also the student's job). In a perfect world, this is done face-to-face in a senior interview. Student and counselor will leave this meeting with a clear sense of what needs to be done, and by when. For about 20 percent of the students, this is the last college meeting they'll need until it's time to talk about financial aid.

Large caseloads may require counselors to have students complete a form instead of attend a meeting. The goal is the same; everyone needs to know what needs to be done, and by when. The requests for appointments will rise significantly the day the form is distributed, and these requests will typically come from students who genuinely need the help. This will last about a week and then die down, making it easy to meet the appointment requests over the first three weeks of school.

Finally, there is the Senior Night program, which will include a review of college application procedures and deadlines, a reminder about the importance of the twenty-minute meeting, and your Paying for College program. You can pull content from recent newsletters, the key points made at the junior parent program in the spring, and anything that changed over the summer. The real goal of this program is to remind, reinforce, and reassure.

Once the first three weeks of school have come and gone, priority attention goes to the students who have not been in touch. In too many cases, they've changed their college plans and are too scared to discuss them, they've never had any college plans and don't want to admit that, or the prospect of leaving high school is suddenly too terrifying to process. Some of these students can be encouraged to see you just because senior year is moving along quickly, but other students will need more coaxing. Seek the help of parents and faculty, if necessary, but touch base with every student by October 1.

Notes and Follow-Up

- It's important to allow ample time in the fall to see as many students as possible in person. To achieve that goal, make a list of all of the activities you're involved in at school from your first day back through mid-October.
    - Which of these activities could be moved to another time of year?
    - Which of these duties are non-counseling duties that could be reassigned?
    - What programs and projects could be supported by volunteers from the Counseling Advisory Committee?
- Review the procedure you use to schedule appointments, and how you communicate this process. Do students have easy access to it? Do parents?
- Many counselors are seeing the benefits of being able to reach their students (especially their seniors) on short notice through a texting program like *Remind*. Look at the Remind website, and list its advantages and disadvantages for your program.

Chapter 43
NO COLLEGE

The exciting tumult of senior year makes it too easy to forget that the goal of the college counseling curriculum is *not* to send every student to college, but to expose all students to the entire array of college options and the benefits of each and help them decide if college is for them. That goal suggests some students will decide to go to college, and some will not.

Just as no counselor should second-guess a student's choice of college, we shouldn't second-guess a student's choice of no college, as long as it's sound. When a student is directly or indirectly questioning the worth of college—especially in senior year—consider these points in your discussion with them:

College cost. Students who tell you college costs too much may not have explored the full range of college and funding options and are likely saying they worry about having to go into debt to pay for college. Since many students still think of college as a four-year experience at one school, check to see if the student has thought about attending a community college, or starting there and transferring to a four-year college. Alternate definitions of college may open the student to options that are more affordable, more appealing, or both.

In terms of debt, students are rightly concerned about the impact of debt on their lives. At the same time, an engineering major graduating with the nation's average of $28,000 in college debt will have little trouble paying that loan off in five years, if they so choose. Not every student is an engineering major, but the best way to get past the statistics is to look at the specifics: where do they want to go, and what do they want to study? Any student concerned about debt needs help doing just that.

Economic benefit. Entrepreneurs and those with special trade skills are being covered by the media as never before, strong examples of the claim that people can make it without a college degree. But is that really the case?

A good number of successful business mavericks may not have a bachelor's degree, but most of them started on the road to success after a year or two at college, where they learned plenty about themselves, if nothing else. As for the skilled-trades workers, many honed their craft in a training program taught through a community college, which is as much of a college experience as the student who goes to medical school. A four-year college may not be for everyone, but some training after college not only makes sense; it makes dollars and cents.

Ability to benefit. Beyond the economic arguments lie the students who most need our help, the students whose talents and interests have never been fully realized or appreciated in school. They see four years of college as more of the same, and they simply don't want to put themselves through that.

It's hard to argue with that viewpoint, so don't. Stop talking college, and start talking about life—their life—and what they want to do, what they want to experience, and what they want in their lives that isn't there now.

These students may or may not need college, but what they most need now is a fresh start, and the confidence to know they're entitled to one. There are plenty of tools in your career curriculum to help them find some answers. One fresh start may ultimately require a college experience, but that doesn't have to come right away; it just has to come when the student is ready for it.

Notes and Follow-Up

- Some students aren't interested in college because they think it will be just like high school. Make a list of reasons why they may be right, and a list of reasons why they're wrong. Put together a newsletter article that addresses this important issue.

- *Earnings and unemployment rates by educational attainment* is an updated report the Bureau of Labor Statistics produces to address the issue of the value of all levels of college. Take a look at this chart, and consider how you would use it as part of your college counseling curriculum.

Chapter 44
WORKING WITH COLLEGE ADMISSIONS OFFICERS

Fall is also the time to schedule college admissions officers for high school visits. Just as colleges want to understand who the applicants are as people, colleges want to understand counselors as people. Strong, clear, consistent communication with the admissions officers who make the visits, read your students' applications, and decide if a student is worth taking a risk on, can benefit everyone.

What are the keys to working effectively with college representatives? A group of admissions officers was asked that question, and their answers fell into three important categories:

Let us get to know you. Admissions representatives will leave half of the high schools they visit never having talked to a school counselor. College reps realize counselors are busy people— they are too—but ten or fifteen minutes can bring you up to date on new programs and scholarship opportunities at the college, while counselors get a chance to give the rep a heads-up on a special student who'll be applying this fall. If there truly is no time, even just a handshake and "thanks for coming" goes a long way.

Help us make the most of our time together. If a school allows all students to attend a college visit, try to make sure they are really interested in learning more about the college and not just getting out of class. Some high schools limit the number of college presentations a student can attend; others require the student to sign up ahead of time, provide a link to the college's website for research before the visit, or post a set of questions in the newsletter or counseling website to ask visiting reps.

If the school only allows colleges to visit during lunchtime, that policy needs to change. College reps would rather not come at all than be left with a table and seven hundred hungry students. That's no place for the student to get a good impression of the college, or the college to get a good impression of the school. If the policy can't change, invite 8-10 colleges to talk with students in the lunchroom. This creates a mini-college fair environment that significantly increases student participation.

Contact us. If reps have a question about a student who has applied to their college, the reps want to feel they can contact the counselor and get an answer as soon as possible. One of the best ways to create that strong level of communication is to do the same thing: call or e-mail a rep with a question about a program or an application. Like counselors, some reps prefer e-mail to calling, so ask them what works for them, and be sure to respond to their questions in a timely manner.

When it comes to sharing specific information about a student—a sudden change in grades, a disciplinary action, personal information—be sure to share that directly, by telephone if possible. Feel free to check the "please contact me" box on the application if you have information that should be shared only on the phone, or for a paper application, simply put a sticky note on the application that says "Call me." They will.

Reps won't be able to admit every student (even the best of the best), and counselors won't always be able to meet with reps who visit your high school, especially if it's Homecoming Week. But building strong communication from the outset can create a basis of support that makes the challenges easier to understand and overcome, and that benefits everyone.

Notes and Follow-Up

- Develop a list of questions you would ask every college admissions officer who visits your school. Consider these:
  - What changes have occurred in programs or buildings at your college?
  - What are the test scores and average GPA of last year's admitted (that's admitted, not applied) students?
  - Do you recompute GPA? If so, how?
  - What advice would you give to juniors and seniors who visit campus?
  - Do you offer special tours for younger students?
  - Do you require or recommend interviews for applicants? If so, what one piece of advice would you give students about to interview?
  - What would you like to know about our students and our high school?
  - Do you prefer the traditional format of letters of recommendation, or are bullet-style letters acceptable?

- Call three college admissions officers who work with your school, and ask them what your school can do to help them serve your students.

- Review the list of colleges your students apply to, and make note of the three most popular colleges that don't visit your high school. Contact them to see if your school can be included on their visit schedule, if only on an every-other-year basis.

- Look at the fall calendar for your high school, and make a list of the days when other events make it wise to avoid scheduling visits from college representatives.

- Consider the way students sign up to meet with the college reps who visit your high school. Is the process accessible? Does it require students to be thoughtful about signing up? How could it be improved?

Chapter 45
APPLICATION STRATEGIES AND DEADLINES

Students applying to many colleges will need to know which applications to work on first. Students may be tempted to start with the application that has the most essays; instead, the order should be driven by when the application needs to be submitted.

This is harder than it looks. Many colleges with a **rolling admissions** process will tell you their deadline is in February. However, rolling admissions works on a "first come, first served" basis, where students usually receive a decision six to eight weeks after applying. Spots fill up quickly at many rolling admissions colleges, making it harder to get admitted the longer the student waits to apply. To be on the safe side, students should plan on submitting rolling admissions applications by October 15.

Colleges with other admissions programs usually have fixed deadlines. An **early action** (EA) program requires a student to submit their application early (usually in November). In exchange, the college will give the student a decision in about eight to twelve weeks, well before the typical notification time of April 1. Students can apply early action to as many colleges as they wish—though not every college offers this option. A handful of US colleges offer an **early action single choice** program that limits the student to applying early action to just that college.

This is very different from students applying to a college's **early decision** program. Also known as ED, this program also has an early deadline (typically November), and the college will notify the student in six to twelve weeks. The big difference is that a student admitted under an early decision program *agrees to attend that college,* and must withdraw applications to all other colleges once they know their ED college can meet their demonstrated financial need. Because of this commitment, students can only apply to one college's ED program at a time.

Variations of these programs exist, so it's wise to look at the EA and ED requirements of every college a student applies to—but the larger question is, why would a student apply to a school under an early program? For some, the answer is security; hearing back from a college as early as December can give these students peace of mind to enjoy the rest of their senior year, knowing they have been admitted to at least a college or two.

Other students apply early (especially ED) because their research shows that a particular college admits a much larger percentage of its early applicants than students applying **regular decision** (typically in January). Some colleges will admit as much as half their class through an ED program, but students need to remember they are improving their chances of admission at the cost of giving up the rest of their college options if they're admitted to their ED school. Counselors will want to work closely with students thinking of applying ED. If the student isn't absolutely devoted to every aspect of the school, they may not want to apply ED.

Most students find they can complete one college application every weekend if they devote one to two hours on Saturday and Sunday to the task. It's best to work on applications on weekends, leaving the week to focus on homework and the active schedule of a busy senior. Since seniors typically apply to anywhere from four to twelve colleges, completing one application each weekend means they can start their applications once school begins, and finish applying no later than Thanksgiving.

Notes and Follow-Up

- Review the admissions deadlines and kind of deadline (EA, ED, rolling) for the twenty-five most popular colleges your students apply to, noting that some colleges have more than one deadline. Create a spreadsheet with this information, post it on your counseling website, and consider posting it in an early edition of your senior and junior newsletters.

- Call the colleges on your list that offer EA and ED, and ask them what percentage of their acceptances were extended to EA and ED students. Add this information to your chart.

Chapter 46
ESSAYS

It's certainly important for seniors to continue to earn strong grades in demanding classes, but much of their academic and social story has already been told in the first three years of high school. There are two places in the application where they get to start fresh: essays, and interviews.

Both parts have the same goal—to get to know the person behind the grades, test scores, and achievements—and students need to be reminded of this frequently. Faced with the task of writing about themselves, students often think they are giving a speech, or talking about themselves the way they would present a book report. In reality, colleges would rather talk to each student on campus for a couple of hours. They can't do that, so instead they ask the student to write their part of the conversation on paper. That is the purpose of the college essay.

Essays fall into three categories. Most **long-essay** prompts seem to ask the student to write either a factual response or a personal response; in fact, most long-essay prompts are looking for a little bit of both. "Reflect on a time when you challenged a belief or idea" (which comes from *The Common Application*) may seem to ask for a recollection of a specific event, but if the student leaves out the context around the challenge, or a description of what else was going on in their life at the time, they're missing out on a chance to give the colleges a full answer—and that's what they want. Like teacher letters, this isn't about answering a question; it's about telling a story. If the admissions officer finishes reading the essay and is surprised when they look up to see the student isn't in the room, the essay has done its job.

It's harder for students to provide a mix of fact and reflection on a **short-answer** question, but that's also the goal. When asked "What books have you read lately?" it's more than fine for the student to add more information, as long as it doesn't take away from the central question. "I went on a bit of a Southern novel streak this summer: *To Kill a Mockingbird* (the 'new' Harper Lee book controversy is fascinating), *The Sound and the Fury* (an iffy teacher recommendation, which took me to) *Absalom, Absalom* (loved!), *Wise Blood,* and the first three Harry Potter books (not Southern, but in a hammock with my sister, every night this summer)." Story told; mission accomplished.

One short question students often overlook is the **Why us?** question. With so many students applying to so many colleges, admissions offices want some assurance that the student has researched the college enough to know it will be a good fit if the college admits the student. Since the limit on this question is often one hundred words or less, too many students write something casual about the school and think they're done. In reality, if the student's answer doesn't show some depth of research and reflection—and if the answer (in this case only) can be used to answer the Why us? question for another college—it's time to start again. Their answer here can be a game changer.

Many students will need encouragement to write more than one draft of an essay, and all parents should be reminded that their involvement in the essay-writing process is limited to giving the student a quiet place to write. Students should show their essays to a grammar- knowledgeable adult, but that should be a teacher, counselor, or tutor— a professional who knows the boundaries of editing.

Notes and Follow-Up

- Not every college accepts The Common Application, but many college's long-essay prompts are similar to *The Common Application essay prompts*. Review these long-essay prompts. What advice would you offer your students as they consider which one to select? (If you aren't familiar with Common App, create an account, and take a tour. Along with the *Universal College Application*, Common App is used by students to apply to many colleges with just one application.)

- Review the essay requirements (long and short answer) of the applications for the ten most popular colleges your students apply to. What are the similarities? What are the differences? Based on this research, what advice would you give to students interested in keeping their essay writing to a minimum? Remember, it's fine to use the same essay for more than one application, as long as it answers each prompt (and the student has changed the name of the college if it's used in the essay).

- Many high schools offer essay-writing workshops for students that address college essays, essays needed for scholarships, and essays that are part of the application for summer programs. Look at your school calendar and see where you could offer this program. Consider which members of your Counseling Advisory Committee, or college admissions officers, could assist with this program.

Chapter 47
INTERVIEWS

While some students panic at the thought of writing a college essay, nearly every student experiences a new level of stress when they're asked to set up a time for a college interview. From what to say to what to wear, students realize this is the first time in their lives they've been interviewed for anything, and the lack of experience too easily pulls them away from the real goal of the activity.

The best way to prepare a student for an interview is to provide general information about interviews to all students through the college counseling curriculum. Giving them the ground rules allows them to relax, so make sure your newsletter or evening program addresses these issues:

- Not every college requires or offers an interview as part of the admissions process.
- Unlike the SAT Subject Tests, if a college says an interview is optional, it really is optional. If you can have one, do it; if it's impossible, it's OK.
- If one is required, the college will contact you to arrange for the interview.
- If you can have either an on-campus interview with a college admissions officer or an off-campus interview

with an alumni interviewer, they will give equal consideration to both. Some will occur by telephone; these are also given equal weight.

- When the college contacts you to set up an interview, respond right away, but schedule the interview to leave time to talk to your counselor first.

- Don't wear jeans.

The good news about interviews is that students will run to the counseling office the moment they are invited to attend one—that's how new this is to them. When this happens, review these six key points; they've heard them before, and this gives them some confidence that they understand what's going on.

Build on this confidence by running them through the chronology of an interview. Arrive fifteen minutes before your interview; this gives you time to get a little lost. Dress professionally: clean clothes, nice slacks, skirt, or business dress. If your shoes can be polished, shine them.

You can bring a resume to the interview, but don't hold it while you're talking; hand it to the interviewer once you shake hands. A good interviewer will ask you a mix of questions about yourself and the college: what are your interests, what current events concern you, what career interests do you have, what did you think of the campus when you visited? It's likely that the interviewer will ask the Why us? question, so be ready to talk specifically about what that college has to offer that makes it special to you.

Feel free to go into some detail with your answers, but know when to stop. One-word answers don't go over well, but neither do three consecutive answers that each last more than two minutes. Like a college essay, you want the interview to show who you are and what matters to you. Do that, and all will go well.

At the end of the interview, you're likely to be asked if you have any questions. Prepare one or two in advance; one can be a general question about the college (alumni reps usually can't answer questions about specific majors), and one can be more personal to the interviewer, such as "What part of the college means the most to you?" If a question comes to you during the interview, ask that too.

The next day, contact the interviewer by e-mail, voice mail, or a handwritten note to thank them for the interview, and invite the person to contact you if they have other questions. Include some highlights from the interview ("I really appreciated that story about your internship"), and you've shown the college who you are.

Notes and Follow-Up

- Make a list of the members of your Counseling Advisory Committee who could help students prepare for interviews. Members of the business community are especially strong candidates, as is the speech teacher.

- Alumni living in the area may be willing to come in and do an informal presentation on interviews. This is especially helpful if they do alumni interviews for their college. Develop a list of local alumni interviewers, and check your October or November calendar for a good time to hold this workshop during the school day.

- Ask the admissions officers who visit your high school if they offer, encourage, or require interviews. What general advice would they give to students before the interview, and what do they see as the one thing every student must do in an interview?

- The clear rule for all admissions interviews—on campus or off, alumni or admissions officer—is that parents may not sit in on the interview. You know why; they may not. Write a one-hundred word article for your newsletter file on this topic.

Chapter 48
COUNSELOR LETTERS

Many colleges look at the counselor letter to introduce the student's application to the admissions office. While teacher letters may describe having that student in one class, the counselor describes having that student in the school. This very tall order becomes more manageable when looking at specific tasks.

Legal. Most Secondary School Reports (SSR) ask a counselor to confirm the student's eligibility to graduate, GPA, rank in class, and other technical information about the school. Most high schools send a profile with each college application, describing the school's curriculum and community; it also includes a list of colleges attended by recent graduates. This gives the college a sense of the learning environment the student is used to.

Establishing context. In addition to class rank and GPA, many colleges ask counselors to compare the applicant to other students, using a check-box method to evaluate personal qualities (leadership, perseverance, etc.). If the counselor is providing a thorough letter, most colleges don't require this section to be completed, as long as the letter offers some indication of the student's academic rigor in course selection, their level of participation and achievement in extracurricular activities, and other characteristics and best qualities that make the student stand out from their peers.

Personalizing context. Counselors also use the letter of recommendation to explain any extenuating circumstances that affected the student's grades, class selection, participation in extracurricular activities, or the student's life in general. Some counselors will use the letter to talk about a student's extensive illness, family hardships, or unusual circumstances, while others will introduce these issues, and ask the college admissions officer to contact the counselor for more information.

The student may want to write about some of these same experiences in their own essays, a decision that could demonstrate considerable honesty and insight on the student's part. The counselor will want to talk with the student about who will address these issues, and how. This helps the counselor write a letter that complements the student's essays. It also gives the counselor an opportunity to help the student write about the issue with a perspective that focuses less on the challenge and more on its resolution.

The format of the letter is usually left up to the counselor, but it should be no more than a page for nearly all students. While most letters are written in paragraph style, a number of colleges are starting to show a preference for **bullet-point letters**, where the counselor highlights the student's accomplishments in a more focused format. Many colleges find this approach does a better job of bringing the student's qualities to life. Regardless of format, the letter should also briefly convey how long the counselor has known the student, and in what capacities.

Like strong teacher letters, counselor letters make the best impression when they convey a story about the student, a moment when the student's exceptional qualities really shone. This story can come from the counselor's direct experience with the student, or (with their permission,) from information someone else has shared with the counselor—including the student.

The counselor naturally wants to portray the student in the best possible light, but it's important to be honest while being supportive. Going beyond an accurate description of the student could lead to the student matriculating to a college that is a poor fit. In addition, it could strain relations between the college and the counselor, as well as the high school, making it more difficult for future qualified students from that high school to be considered for admission to the college.

Notes and Follow-Up

- Review the programs, activities, and appointments in your college counseling curriculum that allow you to interact directly with your students. Combined with any forms the students submit, does your curriculum create enough opportunities for you to construct a well-informed basis for a strong letter of recommendation for every student? If not, consider what could be changed to increase those opportunities.

- Some counselors lack a systematic approach to keeping student notes that would help them construct strong counselor letters. Review the record-keeping methods you use. What would make it easier to keep meaningful notes, especially after a spontaneous interaction with a student?

- Call three admissions officers at colleges that require a counselor letter as part of the admission process. What qualities do they like to see in a letter? What mistakes should be avoided? Are they open to the bullet-point approach to counselor letters?

- Counselor letters are usually classified into three categories: Narrator (simply provides factual information on every student), Advocate (is mildly supportive of every student), and Cheerleader (offers unequivocal support for every student). Read five of the counselor letters you wrote last year. Which category do you see yourself in as a rule, and why might it be important to write from all three of these roles, depending on the student?

Chapter 49
ADMISSIONS DECISIONS

After many years of long planning, seniors have finally applied to college—and now they're hearing back. In a school where many students apply to the same college, counselors may want to see if the admissions rep from that college will provide an advance list or phone call just before decisions are released, so counselors can know which students might need some additional support processing their decision.

Counselors will also want to keep as clear a calendar as possible on days when many decisions will be sent, including the last week in March, when many highly selective colleges send their admissions decisions. Both strategies give you time to help students who may have questions, need advice, or simply want to share their good news. Forms should be ready for students to complete that track every decision and all scholarship money each student receives. This helps future students applying to the same colleges, and it makes end-of-the-year reporting that much easier.

There are four basic kinds of decisions, and each one comes with some follow-up work:

Admitted. The college is offering the student the opportunity to attend, and that's wonderful news. Other information in the admitted letter can include details on housing deposits, scholarships, and orientation—and some of this news may require a response from the student. Make sure the student reads every part of the admit letter carefully, and has a plan to respond on time.

Denied. The deny letter often cites the high number of quality applicants the college received that year, making it impossible for them to offer admission to every qualified student. This is designed to make the student feel better; it usually doesn't. Students who come to you with news of a denial may simply be looking for comfort and support, while others may be looking for advice on what to do next. Be ready for both.

Some will come and ask if they can call the admissions office to find out more about the reason for the denial; most colleges are happy to get those calls. Students who want to appeal a denial are likely to find a challenge. Most colleges don't offer an appeal, and those that do almost never overturn a decision. In most cases, students are better off calling the college to ask the admissions representative why they were denied. If the opportunity exists to provide new or corrected information, the student should do so; that may be enough for the admissions representative to say they will review the student's file.

Waitlisted. Not every student offered admission says yes. If enough turn the college down, the college may need to admit more students than it first thought. This is why some (not all) colleges waitlist students. The message here is if a spot opens up, the college will admit the student.

Waitlisted students need to do more than sit by the mailbox and wait for good news. In addition to telling the college they wish to stay on the waitlist, the student should consider sending the college current grades, information on awards or other notable activities they have been involved in since submitting the application, and possibly an extra letter of recommendation. Some colleges will tell you they don't want any of this extra information; respect that request in those cases.

It's also important students understand that most colleges use the waitlist to meet certain needs. If too many chemistry majors from Oklahoma have turned down an admissions offer, the first students off the waitlist will be chem students from Tulsa. Expressing interest in the school is important once you're waitlisted, but it's only part of the equation.

We'll discuss the fourth kind of decision in the next chapter.

Notes and Follow-Up

- Review the procedures you have in place to receive and record the admissions decisions students receive. Is the current method of data gathering the best way to organize the results, given the reports you generate that use this data? Does it maintain student confidentiality?

- Look at your calendar, and determine when your students receive most of their college decisions. Are there non-college counseling activities held during these peak periods that could be moved, so college-bound seniors could have more time to talk with you about their college plans?

- Review the websites of the five most popular colleges your students apply to. What is the stated policy for filing an appeal of an admission decision at each? Would you share this information with all students or only supply it to students who ask?

Chapter 50
DEFERRALS, AND ADMISSION STRATEGIES

Students often confuse being **deferred** with being put on a waitlist. Deferrals usually occur when a student has applied to a college through an Early Action or Early Decision program, or when they apply to a rolling admissions school. A deferral means the college needs more information before it can make a decision—and that decision may be to put them on a waitlist! Again, some colleges may ask for updated grades and nothing else; if that's what they say, that's what the student does.

If the college has no limits, an extra letter of recommendation, and a brief update of achievements and grades since the student applied, will be perfect. Send these in right away. If a student is deferred in December or January, it's also a good idea to send an update in a brief note in March, or when the college is making final decisions.

Counselors often wonder if it's appropriate to call admissions officers when a student is deferred, waitlisted, or denied—or if they should call to advocate for a student before admissions decisions are even made. As a rule, college admissions officers prefer to initiate contact with a counselor when reviewing a student's application. Counselors who feel the need to offer extra clarification, or to make the college aware of sensitive information, should check the Please Contact Me box on the application, or add a note at the end of the counselor's letter of recommendation asking for a conversation. In nearly every case, the admissions officer will contact the counselor when the file is being reviewed to discuss the student. If the college doesn't initiate contact and a deadline is approaching, it's reasonable for the counselor to get in touch with the college.

Counselor contacts take on a different approach when a student has already received an admissions decision. If a decision leaves the student or the parent with questions, it's best for them to contact the school counselor first; if the family still has concerns, or wants to inquire about an admissions appeal, they should then be referred to the admissions office. This keeps the counselor aware of the family's concerns, without putting the counselor in the middle of a conversation where an intermediary isn't usually helpful.

In some cases, the counselor may decide a student's unique circumstances require the counselor to contact the college. This can include a situation that is sensitive, complex, or not fully understood by the parent or student; concern that the family member's direct contact with the college might adversely affect the student's chances of admission; or when the parent insists the counselor call, and the counselor feels compelled to do so.

Colleges are often swamped with phone calls and e-mails once decisions are released, sometimes making it challenging for the admissions officer to respond in a timely manner. Once contact is made, the counselor should strongly consider advising the college if the only reason they are calling is at the request of the parent. This is especially true if there is no new or additional information to disclose. A follow-up call should not put the counselor's relationship with the college at risk.

There may be some truth to the stories that counselors from certain high schools are free to call some colleges and "campaign" for their students, but counselors should wait to receive an invitation before starting this on their own. Either way, the counselor letter is the best place to support every student's application. Counselors may need to think twice about the long-term consequences of advocating more for some students than others by doing anything else.

Notes and Follow-Up

- Review your process for organizing the names and contact information of your college admissions representatives. How is this information updated, especially for the colleges that are popular with your students?

- Not every college admissions representative welcomes contact directly from parents or counselors. Make a note to ask all admissions officers about their preferences when they visit your high school.

- Prepare a summary of the four kinds of college decisions students receive, and what they need to do once they receive each one. This is likely to take up an entire newsletter edition.

- Review your admissions data from last year for colleges that offer students admission in the summer semester, or January semester. This is becoming more common if a college is full for the fall semester. Would you share this information with seniors when they are applying in the fall?

Chapter 51
PAYING FOR COLLEGE, PART I

The "college is affordable" message that used to be focused on low-income families and parents of first-generation students now has to be shared with a much larger audience, and much earlier in the college awareness curriculum. In some cases, this is the only part of the college counseling curriculum shared in elementary school, and for two reasons. First, students raised in households where they hear the message that college costs too much are more likely to believe it, and lower their expectations and level of preparation for college. Second, parents who want help saving for college need to implement their savings plan early, taking full advantage of what Einstein called the eighth wonder of the world: compound interest.

In using the many resources available to help parents and students understand college costs, it's vital to focus on the idea of paying for college, not financial aid. This small change in phrasing invites more people to the conversation, especially parents who feel college costs too much, but also believe the current system offers no help to the middle class. In their eyes, not everyone qualifies for financial aid, but everyone can get help paying for college.

Conversations about college costs should be specific and attention grabbing. Parents have heard far too many stories of students dropping out of college with six-figure debt to believe any vague message that "your child can go to college." A financial aid officer at a private college begins his presentations by saying, "The cost of attendance at our college is forty-eight thousand dollars, and the average student receives thirty-nine thousand dollars in financial aid, graduating with twelve thousand dollars of debt." By putting the numbers out front, the myth and mystery are taken out of the conversation, and the discussion now changes to how parents can make college that affordable (or even more affordable) for their child.

It's also important to consider who delivers this message to parents. The most effective parent programs on paying for college feature college financial aid officers, who are usually happy to present at high school programs. The rules for financial aid change weekly, if not daily, and a financial aid officer can give parents the most accurate information, based on the latest insights.

Ironically, most parents are also more receptive to sharing at least some of their fiscal situation with a financial aid officer (a complete stranger), and not the school counselor. Part of this is based on perceived expertise, but more of it is likely based on the parents' desire to make sure no one in the local community knows about the parents' finances.

Involving financial aid officers in paying-for-college presentations also goes a long way to breaking down another myth. Too many families complete the required financial aid forms, receive their financial aid award, and accept it without question. They feel this is all they can qualify for, and they have to accept all of it. Involving financial aid officers early in the paying-for-college curriculum shows students and parents that financial aid officers are human, and those involved with it want to help families as much as possible.

Financial aid policies are governed by clear guidelines, but financial aid officers can offer ideas, make suggestions, and use reasonable professional discretion to work with families to create a number of approaches toward paying for college. These conversations can only begin if parents call and ask questions; that is more likely to occur once they know financial aid officers are approachable.

Notes and Follow-Up

- *Studentaid.gov* is the best place to direct parents for an overview of the federal financial aid program and paying for college in general. It includes information on each of the government programs and offers advice on paying back loans. Spend thirty full minutes on this website.

Chapter 52
PAYING FOR COLLEGE, PART II

While it's best to let financial aid officers talk about the latest trends and qualifications for aid, counselors still play a vital role in the paying-for-college curriculum. This includes creating the groundwork for applying for financial aid, and searching for private scholarships.

The counselor will want to make sure families know when to file for federal aid (January for the Class of 2016, any time after October 1 for all others) and state aid (varies by state). Parents will also need to be familiar with important concepts such as **cost of attendance** (tuition, room and board, books, travel from home to campus, personal expenses), **net price calculators** (required to be on each college's website to give parents an estimate of college costs), **expected family contribution** (EFC, the amount parents can pay for college, according to the federal government), and the **Student Aid Report** (SAR, sent by the college to show what financial aid the student will receive).

It's also helpful to tell families ahead of time about some of the current realities of filing for aid:

- Most families feel the EFC grossly overestimates how much they can pay for college.

- Some colleges require additional financial aid forms beyond the FAFSA, such as *CSS Profile** or their own institutional form.

- Colleges structure student award letters differently and don't include the same information (for example, some include merit scholarships, some do not).

- Net price calculators are also structured differently.

- Not all colleges have the resources to meet the family's demonstrated need.

- Many colleges consider the family's ability to pay as part of the admissions process.

- Some colleges offer financial aid based on the college's desire to have a student attend.

- Families can turn down one part of the financial aid offer (such as the loan), while accepting the other parts (such as the grant).

- Financial aid awards can be appealed, leading some families to receive more assistance. Just call!

Because loans are becoming a larger part of the paying-for-college approach families are taking, some counselors discuss the loan options families may qualify for from the federal government, private banks, or both. Other counselors are more comfortable advising families to "watch the loans" and include a banker on their paying-for-college panel.

Counselors will also want to give families real-life examples of students who completed their college goals with the help of reasonable financial aid. Alumni families may not always be willing to share their stories with other community members, but those who are can be invited to participate in the paying-for-college presentation (in person or on tape), write an article for the college newsletter, or be available to talk individually with concerned families.

Families will also need to know when and where to start looking for private scholarship/grant money provided by a funder outside the college that is need-based, merit-based, or both. In addition to providing parents with reliable websites to search for these scholarships, counselors will want to add some words of scholarship advice:

- Some scholarships are open to students in tenth and eleventh grade.

- Some private scholarships and scholarship websites require parents to register by providing their e-mail address and phone number.

- Competition is usually national or international for scholarships promoted on a scholarship search site and could be difficult to receive.

- Never pay to use a scholarship website or apply for a scholarship.

- Never provide a Social Security number to a scholarship company.

- With some modification, students can use the same scholarship essay to apply for multiple scholarships.

- Scholarships requiring teacher letters or transcripts require students to make these requests in advance, just like a college application.

Notes and Follow-Up

- Take a quick peek at *FastWeb, Cappex (for merit aid), Scholly*,* and *Chegg* for scholarship information. The merit aid information on Cappex is hard to find, but is listed by state, so it's worth the hunt.

- Looking for a way to improve FAFSA completion? Look up *MCAN College Cash Completion* and *FAFSA Completion Project.* How can these programs be built into your college counseling curriculum?

- Look up the paying-for-college resources on your state's website. What programs are worth mentioning to your students' parents?

- *Saving plans for colleges* will give you the web results for the latest information on 529 College Savings programs and more. Click on the latest one, and read it. This information changes regularly, so get in the habit of updating yourself.

- If your families use financial planners, make sure they meet to discuss college plans.

- *Avoid Scams Federal Student Aid* gets you back to the federal student aid pages, and talks about some of the don'ts of applying for aid. Take a look, and give it to parents, often.

- Finally—and you knew this was coming—call the financial aid offices of a four-year and two-year college that are popular with your students. Some colleges require parents to file additional forms when applying for financial aid, such as *CSS Profile** or the school's own form.

What forms does each college require? What advice do they give parents? What can counselors do to help parents with financial aid? Specifically, what advice do they give about *PLUS Loans?*

Chapter 53
HELPING STUDENTS DECIDE

When students need help choosing a college, the counselor must resist the temptation to solve "the problem" for the student. Instead, the counselor must create a platform of decision-making based on the student's needs, interests and goals, and explore the components of that platform with the student.

The forms the student completed as part of the junior and senior interviews, combined with counselor notes, can be used to review the student's college process so far. This provides everyone with a clear jumping-off point by asking one simple question: "Is that still what you're looking for, or have things changed?"

This question may knock the student into a profound silence. In the flurry of completing college applications, there's a good chance the student hasn't bothered to think about this question until now. September was eight months and a million adventures ago, so the student may want something different out of college, and not even know it.

In response, the student may not want to talk about qualities; instead, they will try to talk about specific colleges. "Well, I'm really not that interested in State anymore, and East Coast U didn't really offer me that much money, and..."

Drawing on your listening and redirecting skills, bring the student back to the heart of the conversation. "It sounds like affordability is a new quality you're considering. Are there other qualities that are new?" The student may respond with an answer that once again mentions a school by name, but will finally provide the basis for a comparison of schools.

As the comparison reaches a conclusion, the counselor can summarize by saying, "It sounds like your current list of qualities includes affordability, closeness to home, small class size, and opportunities for independent study. If that's right (pause to let them respond), let's talk about each college that admitted you, and compare them on these same qualities."

If a student decides their fall plan for college is no longer viable, it's important to explore the effect this decision will have on those who have a strong interest in the student's decision: the student's parents, the coach, the music teacher, the admissions officer at the school the student was 99 percent sure of, and other members of the community, who can't understand why the student would change their mind. Gaining support (or at least understanding) from others may be vital in order for the new plan to work. Discussing strategies the student can take in approaching these supporters, and even role-modeling practice conversations, could go a long way to help the student.

Similarly, if the student's ideas can change over time, so can the ideas of others, including parents. While Dad was in full support of an out-of-state college in September, he may find letting go of his child is just too hard to do come April, or parental ability to pay for college may have dwindled in eight months. Any number of things can lead to a college decision being made for the student.

174

After helping the student work through any feelings they may have about these changes (or directing the student to someone to help with that), a discussion of college qualities is the best way to help the student focus on the choices at hand, and make the best decision available. It may take time for the student to fully accept the situation, but the counselor's support can go a long way to advance this important goal...and in these times, no discussion about a final choice is complete without a thoughtful discussion double-checking affordability.

Notes and Follow-Up

- Many students who were denied admission to their first-choice college talk about applying for admission there as a transfer student. Search the web using the names of three popular colleges under *Transferring to (College Name Here)* to make sure the student is clear on how likely this might be. In many cases, transfer admission is more difficult than freshman admission.

- Other students will decide they want to attend their first-choice school as a guest student, where they attend for a semester or two and then return to their home college to graduate. Use the same three schools to search for *Attending (College Name Here) as a Guest Student*; this process should be easier.

- Write one-hundred-word articles on each of these topics, and place them in your newsletter file.

- Chapter 55 points out the importance of students sending a deposit to only one college. Read this information and prepare a newsletter article for parents and students to remind them to avoid the temptation to send in more than one deposit.

- Students who want to start their search over again in the spring of their senior year can do so with help from the *NACAC College Openings Update*, which comes out in early May. It lists colleges actively looking for more fall students. Make a note to review this helpful tool every May.

- Other colleges may also welcome applicants. Call the three colleges you've reviewed for guest status and transfer, and ask about their policies on late applicants and students offering to be admitted in the summer or January semesters.

Chapter 54
WRAPPING UP THE PROCESS

After college decisions are made by both the colleges and the students, a few final tasks remain:

Making an enrollment deposit. Students have until May 1 to submit one (and only one) enrollment deposit at the college of their choice. Some colleges give the students longer than this to decide, but no college can give them less time for an enrollment deposit, unless the student applied ED.

Finishing other correspondence. Students need to watch the deadlines outlined in their admissions packet for things such as housing deposits and reserving a day to attend orientation. Colleges aren't supposed to ask for housing deposits before May 1, but many do.

Avoiding summer melt. Research shows a number of students—especially low-income and first-generation students—tell their counselor they're going to college in the fall, but never show up. They're known as summer-melt students. This situation often happens because students aren't in touch with counselors over the summer, and the student loses track of what to do. Counselors are responding to this need for summer information with e-mails, newsletters, phone calls, texts, and in-person meetings in June, July, and August. Your CAC can support these efforts as well.

Notifying colleges. Once students are sure they aren't going to accept a college's offer of admission, they should notify the college in writing. This can be by e-mail or regular letter, and only needs to say "Thank you for your support and offer of admission. I'm declining your offer." Colleges may ask, but there's no need for the student to report where they are going; they just need to send the notification, and they're done.

In some cases, students will know well before May 1 that they aren't going to a particular college. Telling the college early helps it get other students off waitlists—and that could mean the student's best friend gets into college.

Transition to college. More high schools are offering students a college orientation program of their own. Run as a series of lunchtime workshops, an evening program, or a number of newsletters or videos, topics often include money and credit management, college study skills, roommate relations, sexual harassment and violence prevention, and basic laundry skills. Your CAC is a great resource for finding community experts to speak on these topics.

Handling transcript requests. Most high schools have a system where students report all their college admissions decisions and scholarship offers, including the scholarships they didn't accept. Many require students to file this information before graduating—or better yet, before getting graduation tickets.

This information is used to send out final transcripts, which most colleges require before students can matriculate. The form should also have a box that student athletes can check if a copy of their transcript should be sent to the NCAA or another agency.

High schools should organize transcript preparation and printing to make sure final transcripts are sent (preferably electronically) no later than July 1. Since students change their minds, and since transcripts may not get received over the summer, students need to know how to contact the high school over the summer if another transcript needs to be sent, and high schools should have a way to send them quickly during the summer.

National Decision Day. Since many colleges request an enrollment deposit on May 1, many high schools use the occasion to celebrate the postsecondary plans of all of their students, college bound and career bound. These celebrations can include meals, assemblies, parties, and the creation of banners that are displayed to inspire and motivate underclassmen in the coming year.

Notes and Follow-Up

- Ideas for *National Decision Day* include a celebration of the plans of all students, whether they're going to college or not. Do a web search (or review the *MCAN College Decision Day* site) and think about the plusses and minuses of doing something in your school.

- Review your counseling office's plan for student outreach over the summer. Most offices won't publish newsletters, but almost all have to make plans for sending transcripts. Who covers that, and when? Is this important task covered every summer day the school is open?

- New programs on *Summer Melt* are coming together every year. Do a web search, and make a one-hundred-word plan to use your CAC and/or counselors in surrounding areas to implement a summer melt program (and don't forget to remind your students to call financial aid offices to see if other summer melters left any scholarship money behind).

- More colleges are also rescinding offers of admission if a student's grades decline dramatically during senior year. Review your senior newsletters to see how often you share this information, and ask three college representatives what they look for in reviewing final transcripts that could lead to a withdrawal of an offer for admission.

Chapter 55
ETHICS

Is it OK for a college to decide on a student's application for admission based on how much financial aid the student might need? Can a student send an enrollment deposit to more than one college? Can a counselor tell a student one college is just plain better than another?

These are just some of the issues counselors run into when advising students in the college selection process. Given all that's at stake, it's easy to see the need for a set of common rules and standards for counselors, colleges, and families to live by in college admissions, or getting into college would be more chaotic—and expensive—than it is now.

This is why the National Association for College Admission Counseling has the *NACAC Statement of Principles of Good Practice*. Founded in 1937, NACAC is an organization of schools, colleges, companies, and individuals involved in college admissions. NACAC provides a number of services to families and admissions professionals, including *NACAC National College Fairs, NACAC Performing and Visual Arts Fairs,* and myriad professional training opportunities. While NACAC is a member organization, many view the SPGP to be the ethical standard that should be adhered to by everyone in the college admissions field.

The SPGP has three sections:

Mandatory Practices are the actions and activities all NACAC members promise to follow. These practices show that counselors may "not use disparaging comparisons of secondary or postsecondary institutions." It's fine to talk with students about the qualities two colleges have, and let that analysis serve as its own basis of comparison. Anything beyond that begins to violate the SPGP. Members violating these practices can be referred to NACAC's Admission Practices Committee, which can take disciplinary action on the member, up to and including removal from NACAC, and lack of access to NACAC's college fairs.

Interpretations and Monitoring offers clarifications and explanations of the mandatory practices. This section helps members understand the goal of each mandatory practice and often provides examples of appropriate or inappropriate behavior.

Best Practices includes additional behaviors, policies, and programs members should follow, in addition to the mandatory practices. Since best practices are strongly recommended, but not required, members may choose to follow these guidelines, but are not obligated to do so, and they do not risk NACAC disciplinary action if they choose not to follow them. This section states that colleges should "admit candidates on the basis of academic and personal criteria rather than financial need," encouraging colleges not to consider need, but not making the practice an SPGP violation.

What about the student who sends in more than one enrollment deposit? This is covered as a best practice, where "Counseling Members should…(c)ounsel students not to submit more than one admission deposit, which indicates their intent to enroll in more than one institution." It's important to note that this is a best practice, not a mandatory practice, and this recommendation affects the counselor, but not the student.

Since students and parents aren't NACAC members, they aren't subject to discipline by NACAC, but that doesn't mean families are free to do as they wish. Something as simple as double depositing may seem harmless, but this practice has been known to hurt other students, damage college budgets, and have an indirect effect on tuition.

NACAC's Student Rights and Responsibilities (2012) gives families a clear summary of how they should expect to be treated by colleges, and how families should treat colleges in return. With everyone following the letter and the spirit of the SPGP, students are able to make better, well-informed college choices.

Notes and Follow-Up

- This chapter may be coming at the end of the book, but ethics is woven throughout the college counseling curriculum. That's why you need to take the time to read the entire NACAC SPGP and NACAC Student Rights and Responsibilities (2012).

- Now is also the time to review the ethical guidelines of any other counseling associations you are part of or licensed by.

- And while the SPGP encourages colleges not to consider financial need as a condition of admission, many do. Ask the admissions representatives who visit your high school if their college takes ability to pay into consideration, or if it is "need blind."

Chapter 56
PROGRAM EVALUATION

With awards assembly, graduation, and scheduling already on their plates, counselors are hesitant to add program evaluation of the college counseling curriculum to their list of end-of-the year duties. That's understandable, but the data going into the end-of-the-year report doesn't all have to be generated at the end of the year. With some advance planning, data gathering can be an ongoing, and almost unnoticed, activity, while still following the essential rules of evaluation.

As previously mentioned, most high schools already gather the outcomes portion of the data, by asking students to submit the results of all college applications, and any scholarships they may have earned. While this data is usually self-reported, counselors have little other choice but to rely on the integrity of their students, since few colleges send admissions reports to colleges and almost no colleges send scholarship reports on students. Making submission of this information a requirement to get their physical diploma is enough to encourage most students to provide timely, accurate answers.

It's easy enough to gather data for individual components of the college counseling curriculum with a quick survey after each evening program or workshop. Getting an idea of how supported the student felt throughout the process is trickier: Will a student or parent only see the process as a success if the student is admitted to their first-choice school?

Many high schools see an advantage to collecting this information from students and parents well before most college admission decisions come out, sometimes as early as February. This requires students to think more about the college counseling process, and less about the college counseling product. Counselors who see the process and product as one and the same thing will wait until May to distribute their survey.

In constructing evaluation tools, counselors want to focus on the respondent's behavior, as well as their feelings. Before asking, "Was your counselor helpful in your college search?" you should ask, "How many times did you meet with your counselor about college?" The question "How helpful was Senior College Night?" should only come after "Did you attend Senior College Night?" This two-step approach goes a long way to keeping answers in perspective—and you'll get a better understanding of who's using your services, who isn't, and what you can do to improve services to both.

Counselors also want to make sure the questions are student centered when surveying parents or teachers. If counselors want to know how supported parents felt through the process, they should ask that, but that's a different question from "How well do you think the counseling program supported your child through the college selection process?" The same is true when surveying teachers. If the goal is to find out how to best support their letter-writing process, focus on their feelings. If the goal is to find out what students are telling them about the college counseling process, focus on their perceptions of the student's feelings.

Finally, counselors need to consider the format they use to report the findings of their evaluation. Reports that start with the list of college acceptances and scholarship dollars will never be read past the first few pages. Reports that start with a summary of student and parent perceptions of the college counseling process stand a reasonable chance of getting some attention, as readers search for the college and scholarship list. Putting process (and the plans for improvement) first offers the best chance that administrators, the CAC, and the community will support the counselor's plan for growth, a priority that's in everyone's best interest.

Notes and Follow-Up

- It's time to put together your end-of-the-year survey.
  - What data do you want from students—how many times they met with you, how many colleges they applied to, admissions results, scholarships earned, e-mail address for future contact, etc.?
  - What perceptions do you want from students—which programs were most helpful, which were least helpful, what programs should be added, how accessible was the counselor, how could the counselor be more helpful?
  - Don't forget the most important question: "If there is one thing the college counseling program should do to improve, it should be _____."
  - Consider the same issues for parents, alumni, and for teachers supporting students.

186

○ Review all of your evaluation methods with your College Advisory Committee each spring. How can the committee urge community members to complete the survey? What results should be shared with your CAC, and the community in general?

Chapter 57
ONGOING PROFESSIONAL DEVELOPMENT

College counseling is one of the most rapidly changing parts of the counseling curriculum. Application requirements and admit rates can change overnight at some colleges, and so can the application trends of students, as new colleges become the hot place to be. Keeping up is important and doesn't have to be a full-time job, or cost you a fortune. Consider these activities for making sure your college knowledge is fresh and your college counseling curriculum is up-to-date.

Online. Many counselors find it hard to get out of the building, which is why many groups offer online workshops and conferences to keep counselors current without making them travel. Some organizations will charge a fee for participating in their seminar, but allow counselors to view archived workshops for free, so keep an eye out for discounts.

Cyberspace also offers free group lists and blogs where counselors can ask questions of colleagues, and interact with others who also have questions. These sites connect counselors to experiences and resources they otherwise would never have access to. Best of all, there's never a specific time you have to log in to participate.

College tours for counselors. There's no better way for students to understand a college than to visit the campus, and the same is true for high school counselors. Groups of colleges all over the country offer tours for counselors throughout the year, from the COWS tour in Wisconsin to the Florida tour in winter, and much, much more. In addition, counselors can visit individual colleges at just about any time. Call the college several weeks ahead, and they'll be happy to help you plan your visit.

Local counselor groups. Many high school counselors will meet regularly with colleagues from the other high schools in their area, or in their athletic league. These informal meetings are excellent ways to discuss local and state issues of concern (both about college and other counseling topics) without involving cost or excessive travel time. Schools take turns hosting the meetings, which usually occur three to four times a year.

Conferences. If you're fortunate enough to have a principal who understands that the best way to serve a school is to get away from it every now and then, a host of good conferences await you. Both *ACT's fall update* and *College Board's fall update* give counselors the latest information on testing trends and services for their state. College Board also hosts regional programs and *College Board Forum*, where participants look at college trends from a broader perspective.

College counseling workshops and conferences are also offered by *affiliates of the National Association for College Admission Counseling.* While programs and services differ for each of the twenty-three affiliates, each one has an annual conference, many have summer programs for new and experienced counselors, and most programs meet continuing education requirements. NACAC affiliates also help counselors apply for *NACAC*

Imagine Grants, funds that can be used for programs or conference attendance, including the *NACAC Annual Conference**, held in the fall. Membership in NACAC and an NACAC affiliate open counselors to even more professional development opportunities.

Many counselors who need professional development funds have also found support from their local parent-teacher group, or their Counseling Advisory Committee. Some counselors have established newfound support for their program by visiting college campuses with their principal, and meeting with alumni on campus to discuss what the high school can do to improve college readiness. The interest in college has never been higher; now is the time to take full advantage of that interest, and move your college counseling program forward.

Notes and Follow-Up

- A nice list of *College Tours for Counselors* is on PB Works. Look at the list, and check your calendar to see which of these tours will fit into your schedule. Make a note to talk with your principal about this important opportunity; advance notice can help them find funding for visits and work around your travel schedule if necessary.

- If you have local colleges that aren't on the PB Works list, call them and ask if they offer counselors tours. Once you set a date, notify the alumni attending the college that you'd like to buy them lunch, and bring your principal with you. This is a great way to get feedback on your high school's college counseling curriculum and see a college at the same time.

- *NACAC affiliates* takes you to the list of state and regional partners of the National Association for College Admission Counseling. Click on the link of the affiliate that serves your area, and look at its professional development opportunities. If you don't see any, contact the Professional Development chair of the affiliate for more information.

- School counselors looking for additional credentialing in college counseling should look at the requirements for becoming a Certified Educational Planner through the *American Institute of Certified Educational Planners*. Considered by many to be the gold standard for independent college counselors, the CEP credential may come in handy for school counselors who want to solidify their position, and their credibility.

- Write down your top five goals for professional development in college counseling, and do web searches for each of them. Make a list of the webinars and conferences that address this issue, and consider taking a funding proposal to your Counseling Advisory Committee for support.

- If you're interested in online resources to keep in touch with other school counselors try these resources:
  - *High School Counselor Week.*
  - *NACAC Exchange.*
  - On Twitter:
    - #scchat (school counselors).
    - #escchat (elementary counselors).
    - #mscchat (middle school counselors).
    - #hsschat (high school counselors).

- #ReachHigher (White House Initiative on College Access).
  - On Facebook:
    - Elementary School Counselor Exchange.
    - Creative Elementary School Counselor.
    - Caught in the Middle School Counselors.
    - The Middle School Counselor.
    - High School Counselors' Network.
    - College Admissions Counselors.
    - Women in College Admission Counseling.
    - The Counseling Geek.

Chapter 58
BRINGING IT TO LIFE

At the beginning of this book, the section "A Word about Initiating Change" invited readers to list the five goals they would like to develop for their college counseling program and modify that list as they read through the book. Now that the end of the book is near, many readers who took up that challenge are looking at their list, and wondering if they're biting off more than they can chew.

For those readers who aren't sure about their list—and for readers who simply want to get started—the following three-year plan provides an outline that's easy to follow, at least in theory. The schedule for each year is based on the counselor's ability to carve out and keep thirty minutes of planning time for the college counseling curriculum every school day. Since urgent events sometimes dictate flexibility in every counselor's schedule, most of the scheduled tasks can be achieved with three weeks of planning, allowing the counselor one or two periods to engage in more pressing matters.

Schools running an August-to-May schedule should follow the months in parentheses. The chapter related to each activity is in the parentheses found in each activity cell.

Year One

Month	Monday	Tuesday	Wednesday	Thursday	Friday
September (August)	Schedule and prepare for college rep visits (44)	Data review: data you have, data you need (1)	Newsletter (Senior) (7)	Newsletter (Jr/Soph/Jr/Fresh) (7)	Senior Night and Paying for College prep/PSAT 11 prep (42, 21)
October (September)	College Cash Campaign, and Scholarship Review (5/52)	College Application Week prep and implementation (5)	Newsletter (Senior) (7)	Newsletter (Jr/Soph/Jr/Fresh) (7)	Essay Workshop prep and implementation (46)
November (October)	Website review and update (8)	Develop Counseling Advisory Committee (6)	Newsletter (Senior) (7)	Newsletter (Jr/Soph/Jr/Fresh) (7)	Interview Workshop prep and implementation (47)
December (November)	Twenty-Minute Meeting Plan (39)	Plan Tenth Grade College Night for January (15)	Newsletter (Senior) (7)	Newsletter (Jr/Soph/Jr/Fresh) (7)	Plan Junior Night for January and Junior Survey (25)
January (December)	Junior Interviews (23)	Junior Interviews (23)	Newsletter (Senior) (7)	Newsletter (Jr/Soph/Jr/Fresh) (7)	Review PSAT 11 results and Junior Survey results (21)
February (January)	Website review and update (8)	Data review: achievement gaps and undermatching (10, 29)	Newsletter (Junior) (7)	Newsletter (Sr/Soph/Sr/Fresh) (7)	Review evals of Senior and Junior Nights, Paying for College, CAW (56)

March (February)	Implement and review testing (16, 17)	Testing (16, 17)	Newsletter (Junior) (7)	Newsletter (Sr/Soph/ Sr/Fresh) (7)	Testing (16, 17)
April (March)	Begin Annual Report (56)	Plan College Decision Day for May (5)	Newsletter (Junior) (7)	Newsletter (Sr/Soph/ Sr/Fresh) (7)	Plan College Counseling Class for Juniors (58)
May (April)	Professional Development Plan for next year (57)	Data review/ End-of-Year Report (56)	Newsletter (Junior) (7)	Newsletter (Sr/Soph/ Sr/Fresh) (7)	Program evaluation—Seniors and parents (56)

It should come as no surprise that most of year one is spent initiating new programs. Two of the planning periods are devoted to the creation of the newsletters for all grades. As outlined in chapter 7, newsletters for ninth and tenth graders are published monthly for the entire school year. Senior newsletters are published weekly for the first half of the year, and every other week in the second half, while the junior newsletter is the exact opposite. This schedule requires the counselor to produce two newsletters every week.

Some of the planning time is also allotted for implementation of a program. For example, the college essay workshop in October will likely require only an hour to plan, leaving the rest of the planning time for running the workshop. In other cases, such as the development of the Counseling Advisory Committee, the planning time is allotted only for planning; the actual meetings will have to be scheduled at some other time.

Since testing can be an all-consuming activity for counselors, most of the planning time in March is given over to spring testing, which is common in most states. Where testing occurs in a different month, counselors should switch the planning activities to March, freeing the appropriate month for testing.

The only new item on the schedule is "Plan College Counseling Class for Juniors." Many high schools are offering an elective course taught by school counselors, where they engage juniors in many aspects of the college counseling curriculum, including research on colleges, essay writing, scholarship searches, interview skills, and practice in application completion. This course is especially popular in high schools with block schedules that allow the class to meet only once or twice a week. Other high schools will use homeroom or advisory periods for this instruction, which are led by the homeroom teacher or adviser. Still other high schools offer a similar class for seniors, creating a weekly space in the first semester for them to complete college and scholarship applications.

Year Two

Month	Monday	Tuesday	Wednesday	Thursday	Friday
September (August)	Schedule and prepare for college rep visits (44)	Develop ninth and tenth grade curriculum (12, 13, 15)	Newsletter review (all grades) (7)	College Fair planning (20)	Senior Night and Paying for College prep/PSAT 11 prep (42, 21)
October (September)	Update and review College Advisory Committee (6)	College Application Week prep and implementation (5)	Newsletter review (all grades) (7)	College Cash Campaign, and Scholarship Review (5/52)	Essay Workshop prep and implementation (46)

196

November (October)	Website review and update (8)	Review existing programs	Newsletter review (all grades) (7)	College Handbook development (58)	Interview Workshop prep and implement (47)
December (November)	Data review: data storage and external reports (1, 2)	Plan Tenth Grade College Night for January (15)	Newsletter review (all grades) (7)	Review existing programs	Plan Junior Night for January and Junior Survey (25)
January (December)	Junior Interviews (23)	Junior Interviews (23)	Newsletter review (all grades) (7)	Update Summer Program List (14)	Review PSAT 11 results and Junior Survey results (21)
February (January)	Website review and update (8)	Review resources for students with learning differences (31)	Newsletter review (all grades) (7)	Review existing programs	Review evaluations of Senior Night, Junior Night, Paying for College, CAW (56)
March (February)	Implement and review testing (16, 17)	Testing (16, 17)	Newsletter review (all grades) (7)	Develop Middle School College counseling Program (11)	Testing (16, 17)
April (March)	Begin Annual Report (56)	Plan College Decision Day for May (5)	Newsletter review (all grades) (7)	Review existing programs	Review College Counseling Class for Juniors (58)
May (April)	Professional Development Plan for next year (57)	Data review/End-of-Year Report (56)	Newsletter review (all grades) (7)	Evaluate administrative support (9)	Program evaluation—Seniors and parents (56)

The biggest change in the Year Two schedule is the reduction of time devoted to newsletters. As chapter 7 points out, once newsletters have been developed for an entire year, the sequence of information that goes to each grade generally stays the same. This means newsletters only need to be reviewed for changes in any dates that are mentioned; this requires less time.

Time that was devoted to newsletters in Year One is now replaced with development of other new programs, as well as the review and modification of other programs initiated in Year One. Some planning time is required to update programs on a regular basis, while other programs may need a review every one or two years. The review time allows counselors to scan all programs four to five times a year to see what changes and updates, if any, need to be made.

Year Two also includes the first planning time to focus on services given to a special population—in this case, students with learning differences. Time to develop services for other special populations is scheduled in Year Three.

Year Three

Month	Monday	Tuesday	Wednesday	Thursday	Friday
September (August)	Schedule and prepare for college rep visits (44)	Develop Faculty Letter-Writing Workshop (41)	Newsletter review (all grades) (7)	Develop NCAA Program (32)	Senior Night and Paying for College prep/PSAT 11 prep (42, 21)
October (September)	Update and review College Advisory Committee (6)	College Application Week prep and implementation (5)	Newsletter review (all grades) (7)	College Cash Campaign, and Scholarship Review (5/52)	Essay Workshop prep and implementation (46)

November (October)	Website review and update (8)	Review existing programs	Newsletter review (all grades) (7)	Develop Resources for Artists (33)	Interview Workshop prep and implementation (47)
December (November)	Data review: all components (1-3)	Plan Tenth Grade College Night for January (15)	Newsletter review (all grades) (7)	Review existing programs	Plan Junior Night for January and Junior Survey (25)
January (December)	Junior Interviews (23)	Junior Interviews (23)	Newsletter review (all grades) (7)	Update Summer Program List (14)	Review PSAT 11 results and Junior Survey results (21)
February (January)	Website review and update (8)	Develop resources for undocumented students (34)	Newsletter review (all grades) (7)	Review existing programs	Review evaluations of Senior Night, Junior Night, Paying for College, CAW (56)
March (February)	Implement and review testing (16, 17)	Testing (16, 17)	Newsletter review (all grades) (7)	Develop resources for LGBTQ students (35)	Testing (16, 17)
April (March)	Begin Annual Report (56)	Plan College Decision Day for May (5)	Newsletter review (all grades) (7)	Review existing programs	Review College Counseling Class for Juniors (58)
May (April)	Professional Development Plan for next year (57)	Data review/End-of-Year Report (56)	Newsletter review (all grades) (7)	Develop resources for international students (36)	Program evaluation—Seniors, parents, alumni, and faculty (56)

Year Three introduces planning time to develop programming and services for the remaining special populations, as well as a workshop on writing letters of recommendation for the faculty. Data reviews are now more comprehensive, and program evaluation is expanded to include evaluations of alumni and faculty views of the college counseling program.

By the conclusion of year three, most high schools will develop their own planning schedule, keeping those elements that require annual attention, and using the remaining planning periods either to review existing programs, or create new programs based on the results of data and program evaluation.

The Best Gift

She wasn't usually this nervous when she came in my office, so I wasn't quite sure what to expect. She sat down slowly, and said she hadn't heard from her top-choice college, and it had been six weeks (she'd applied to a rolling admissions school).

This was back in the days when a counselor could call a college, give the admissions office a student's Social Security number (don't even think of doing this today), and get a report on the student's status. As I called, I knew what the college would say, and sure enough, I was told she'd been admitted, and would get her letter in the mail in the next few days (like I said, this was a while ago).

I had a big caseload and a busy day ahead of me, so I turned toward my file—and away from the student—to update her record. "Congratulations," I said over my shoulder, "you're in."

I began writing in her record when I heard the smallest of sounds—the one all counselors know by instinct. I turned to find tears running down her cheeks, and all she could say was "Really?"

That moment stayed with me forever. After that, whenever I was privileged enough to give a student admission news, I looked them in the eye, let them know how wonderful this news was, and offered to let them call their parents (right—no cell phones back then either). If they took me up on the offer, I always left the office. This wasn't my moment; it was theirs.

I'm rarely the first to know an admissions decision anymore, but the students who come by to give me the news, good or bad, always thank me for everything I've done.

That's the best gift a counselor can receive. You come in early every day, run a college counseling program, see all kinds of students and lots of them, support their college interests in ways they never know about, encourage them, inspire them, scold them, do things for them they should really do for themselves, make notes of what you need to do before you see them again, go home late, and lie awake thinking about what else you can do to make this easier for them.

It's a lot of work, and while they don't know everything you do, they have some vague idea it's more than they realize, so they thank you with a depth that expresses both what they know, and what they don't know. That isn't just manners, or the right thing to do; that's gratitude, a feeling that is too rarely experienced in the teenage years, one that points to a greater purpose to life than gratification and suggests that, while high school was awesome, there really may be something to living an adult life after all.

Their best gift of thanks to us only comes once we give the best gift of growth to them—and the college counseling curriculum is the means that creates that growth.

I hope this book helps you create an impeccable gift of growth for every student.

A Reminder about Website References (Again)

(This note also appears in the front of the book, but asterisks often send people scurrying to the back of the book to see what they mean.)

Counselors love websites, and rightfully so. With college trends and admission requirements changing so quickly, access to the latest information is a must, and so is understanding the value of every website in its right context.

Footnotes and end notes don't always make for smooth reading, and putting a full-blown web address in the middle of a paragraph isn't really the answer either. That's why any web reference in the book is in italics; if you type the italicized phrase in a web search, the link to the site you need will almost undoubtedly be the first result of the search.

Since school counselors are on tight budgets, the product and information on most every website referenced in the book can be accessed for free. The handful of resources that are fee-based have an asterisk (*) at the end of the reference. Leave the * out when you're completing the search, and you should be all set.

O'Connor Counseling Support Questionnaire

Directions: Each of these statements relates to some aspect of your work as a school counselor. Read each one, and circle the number that best indicates the degree to which you agree with the statement:

     5 = You strongly agree with the statement.

     4 = You agree with the statement.

     3 = You are neutral toward the statement, or you sometimes agree and sometimes disagree with the statement.

     2 = You disagree with the statement.

     1 = You strongly disagree with the statement.

	Strongly Agree	Agree	Neutral	Disagree	Strongly Disagree
1. My principal devotes the necessary time, staff and resources for the implementation of counseling programs and activities.	5	4	3	2	1
2. My principal provides the time, staff, and re- sources for the review, evaluation, and devel- opment of counseling activities.	5	4	3	2	1

	Strongly Agree	Agree	Neutral	Disagree	Strongly Disagree
3. My principal provides the time, staff, and resources necessary for the preparation and follow-up duties that accompany counseling programs and activities (processing paperwork, reviewing files, phone calls, consultations, etc.)	5	4	3	2	1
4. My principal assigns me only duties relevant to my work as a counselor.	5	4	3	2	1
5. My principal provides resources and opportunities for professional development of counselors.	5	4	3	2	1
6. My principal promotes counselor-initiated activities in the classroom.	5	4	3	2	1
7. My principal promotes school-wide counseling programs (assemblies, speakers, etc.)	5	4	3	2	1
8. My principal takes the time to update his/her understanding of the duties and functions of counselors.	5	4	3	2	1
9. My principal seeks and welcomes information from counselors on school, community, and professional issues.	5	4	3	2	1
10. My principal keeps counselors informed of school, community and professional issues that might impact the work of counselors.	5	4	3	2	1

	Strongly Agree	Agree	Neutral	Disagree	Strongly Disagree
11. My principal keeps in touch with me on a regular basis.	5	4	3	2	1
12. My principal encourages an atmosphere of open communication with me.	5	4	3	2	1
13. My principal expresses appreciation to counselors.	5	4	3	2	1
14. My principal appropriately involves counselors in building-wide planning, problem-solving, and decision-making activities.	5	4	3	2	1
15. My principal appropriately involves counselors in long-range planning.	5	4	3	2	1
16. My principal effectively utilizes my resources as a counselor.	5	4	3	2	1
17. My principal promotes the work of counselors to other faculty and staff.	5	4	3	2	1
18. My principal promotes the work of counselors to parents and the community.	5	4	3	2	1
19. My principal promotes the work of counselors to the superintendent and other members of the central office staff.	5	4	3	2	1

	Strongly Agree	Agree	Neutral	Disagree	Strongly Disagree
20. My principal supports counseling decisions when those decisions are appealed to the principal by those affected by the decisions (parents, students, teachers, etc.)	5	4	3	2	1
21. The office space and room needed for counseling activities are available and accessible.	5	4	3	2	1
22. The lighting, painting, and furniture needs of the offices and rooms used by counselors are maintained at appropriate levels.	5	4	3	2	1
23. The technology needs of the department (phones, computers, etc.) are maintained at appropriate levels.	5	4	3	2	1
24. My principal gives me appropriate flexibility in my role as a counselor.	5	4	3	2	1
25. My principal has reasonable expectations for my work as a counselor.	5	4	3	2	1
26. My principal sees me as capable.	5	4	3	2	1
27. My principal trusts my judgment.	5	4	3	2	1
28. My principal demonstrates respect to me as a counselor.	5	4	3	2	1
29. My principal demonstrates respect to me as a person.	5	4	3	2	1

Please provide brief answers to these four questions:

1. My principal best supports my efforts as a counselor by:

2. My principal could best improve support of counseling by:

3. The area of counseling that needs more administrative support is:

4. The area of counseling that is receiving the most administrative support is:

Tally and analysis

1. Copy the scores from questions 1 to 4 below and average them:

_____ + _____ + _____ + _____ = _____ divided by 4 = _____

This score represents the degree of **program and logistical support** you feel you receive from your administration, or the ability of the administration to supply the resources necessary for complete implementation of all facets of a traditional counseling curriculum, including counseling curriculum development, program implementation, and program evaluation.

2. Copy the scores from questions 5 to 7 below and average them:

_____ + _____ + _____ = _____ divided by 3 = _____

This score represents the **encouragement of program growth** you receive from your administration, or the encouragement you receive to expand the use of school-wide counseling activities and for counselors to engage in professional development in order to stay abreast of new trends in the field.

Copy the scores from questions 8 to 20 below and average them:

_____ + _____ + _____ + _____ + _____ + _____ + _____
+ _____ + _____ + _____ + _____+ _____ + _____ = _____
divided by 13 = _____

This score represents the **engaged advocacy** your administration demonstrates by showing awareness and consideration of the needs and purposes of the counseling program by communicating effectively and regularly with counselors, and by keeping the counseling program in mind when completing regular administrative tasks, such as problem solving, goal setting, and communication with external audiences.

4. Copy the scores from questions 21 to 23 below and average them:

_____ + _____ + _____ = _____ divided by 3 = _____

This score represents the ability of your administration to dedicate **capital allocations** to support the physical plant and technological needs that will create a counseling area that is fresh, updated, welcoming, and functional.

5. Copy the scores from questions 24 to 29 below and average them:

_____ + _____ + _____ + _____ + _____ + _____ = _____
divided by 6 = _____

This score represents administrative **affirmation**, or the trust the administration demonstrates in the judgment and abilities of the counselors, shown in the degree of autonomy the principal provides and the tenor of the principal/counselor work relationship.

Next steps

Compare the scores of the five areas of administrative support. Which ones are highest? Lowest?

How do these answers compare to your written answers to the questions on page four?

As you think about administrative support, what is the one thing you would want your administration to do to increase its support of your counseling program, and what would you need to do to get that support?

The next steps you take with this information are really up to you. You could have all of the counselors in your school complete the questionnaire and discuss the results.

You could consider if you want to share the results of the questionnaire with your administrator, and if so, how? In a one-on-one meeting or as part of a counseling department meeting? As you consider this question, remember that average numbers don't tell a complete story, so you probably don't want to simply send your "scores" in a memo or e-mail, and you may not even want to share the scores at all. Instead you may want to focus on the ideas you've generated based on the scores, since the real goal is to improve administrative support of your program, not to use the scores as a trophy or a stick.

Counselors know the limits of test results and how numbers can often make people feel boxed in. If you have a sense that your administrators might respond this way to the results of the questionnaire, it's best to talk about the issues behind the scores and not the scores themselves.

If you have other questions, comments, or ideas on how the OCSQ can be used with administrators, please send them to collegeisyours@comcast.net